ISBN: 9781313163699

Published by:
HardPress Publishing
8345 NW 66TH ST #2561
MIAMI FL 33166-2626

Email: info@hardpress.net
Web: http://www.hardpress.net

The

Art of Reading Latin

W. G. HALE

GINN & COMPANY

THE

ART OF READING LATIN:

HOW TO TEACH IT.

BY

WILLIAM GARDNER HALE,
PROFESSOR OF LATIN IN CORNELL UNIVERSITY.

BOSTON:
PUBLISHED BY GINN & CO.
1887.

I dedicate this paper to JOHN WILLIAMS WHITE *and*
JAMES B. GREENOUGH, *to the influence of whose*
methods of teaching any welcome that may
be given it will be in good part due.

PREFACE.

THE method of teaching herein advocated started, many years ago, from a desire to know Latin literature, and an impatience with the actual amount of reading power attained by a college course. At the outset there existed a conviction that the modern mind could not be so degenerate as to be incapable of reading Latin as the Romans read it, that is to say, in the Roman order, in the Roman medium, and at a rate of speed which would not be intolerably slow in the reading of a modern tongue. The nature of the aim dictated the method to be employed; and the employment of the method proved the soundness of the original conviction.

The writer has for some years intended to publish an account of this method, as it has shaped itself in practical experience with successive classes. First, however, he desired to present it orally before a number of gatherings of teachers. As a beginning, accordingly, the address with which the pamphlet opens was read before the Holiday Conference of the Associated Academic Principals of the State of New York, held in Syracuse in December last. The interest with which the paper

was received was so kindly, and the requests that it be
published without further delay were so pressing, that
it seemed best not to hold to the former intention.

The pamphlet has not the form which was first
intended, namely, that of plain exposition; for, in
spite of the iteration of the personal pronoun, the
form of direct appeal and explanation natural to an
address proved to have its advantages. It has been
necessary, however, to add to the address a considerable supplement.

Though no explicit suggestions will be found in regard to the teaching of Greek, the substance of the
method of course applies alike to either language.

I am under a debt to many of my students of recent
years, whose support of the method, though it was
taken up by them under the sore necessity of an entire
revolution of confirmed mental habits, has supplied me
with the confidence that comes from concrete results.
But I am under especial obligations to my sister, Miss
Gertrude Elisabeth Hale, both for suggestions made
earlier as a result of her own experience (the device
mentioned on page 31 originated, so far as my own
case goes, with her) and for a searching criticism of the
proof of the present pamphlet, from the point of view
of a preparatory teacher.

ITHACA, April 18, 1887.

THE ART OF READING LATIN:

HOW TO TEACH IT.

An Address delivered before the Associated Academic Principals of the State of New York, Dec. 28, 1886.

THE attacks which have been made of late upon the study of Greek and to some extent upon the study of Latin have had at their backs the conviction that the results obtained are very much out of proportion to the years of labor spent upon these languages by the schoolboy and the college student. The danger which threatens classical study to-day in this country is due in large part to the fact that this conviction is a sound one. If the case were different, if the average college graduate were really able to read ordinary Greek and Latin with speed and relish, the whole matter would be on a very different footing from that on which it now lamely stands.

To learn to read Greek and Latin with speed and relish, and then, if one's tastes turn towards literature or art of any kind, to proceed to do so; to come to know familiarly and lovingly that great factor in the record of the thinking and feeling of the human race, the literatures of Greece and Rome, — that is an aim which we should all set before our students. But, speaking generally, our students, yours and mine, do not come to love those literatures. Perhaps they tolerate them, perhaps they respect them. But to love them and to make them a substantial part of the intellectual life, — that is a thing which many a student, fitted therefor by natural taste and ability, fails to accomplish, and never so much as knows his loss. This seems to me, looking at the long years of study given to Greek and Latin, and the great emphasis put upon them in the requirements for admission to our colleges, a very sad business.

Now the blame of it all must be divided among three parties, — the Greek and Latin languages themselves, the teachers in the preparatory schools, and the teachers in the universities. The first of these guilty parties are out of our reach. They are difficult languages; but difficult languages they must remain. That leaves the practical whole of the responsibility to be divided between the teachers in the preparatory schools and the teachers in the universities, or, to take concrete examples, for the purpose of our conference, between you and me.

Which of us is the more to blame, I will not attempt to say. But so much I will say, and from my sure observation: that the influence upon the formation of intellectual character exerted by the teachers who prepare young men for college is nearly ineffaceable. The boy who comes to college with a thinking habit is capable of learning to read Latin (for I must now confine myself to that topic, though the whole substance of what I have to say applies with equal force to the teaching of Greek) with ease and speed; the boy who comes without the habit has faults that a college course can rarely cure. That the boy should be taught to *think* before he comes to college is, then, from the point of view of the study of Latin, the one indispensable thing. That it is so from every other point of view as well, makes our case so much the stronger.

But one thing more is also indispensable sooner or later for a high success (and there is in Latin but one success), namely, that the method which the boy is taught to use in his thinking be the *right* one, — the result of the most careful observation of the practical difficulties to be overcome, and the most careful study of the best ways of overcoming them.

As we group these difficulties, placing them in the order in which they would be felt by a beginner, we find them to be : —

1. The vocabulary.
2. The system of inflections.
3. The elaborate use of this system of inflections to express meaning, in place of our simpler modern methods of using prepositions, auxiliaries, and the like; or, in a single word, *syntax.*

I suppose the beginner would think that these three difficulties covered the whole ground, and that if he had his vocabulary and his inflections secured, and understood what is called syntax, he could then read Latin with great ease. But he would be very wrong. The most formidable difficulty has not been mentioned. The Latin sentence is constructed upon a plan entirely different from that of the English sentence. Until that plan is just as familiar to the student as the English plan, until, for page after page, he takes in ideas as readily and naturally on the one plan as on the other, until, in short, a single steady reading of the sentence

carries his mind through the very same development of
thought that took place in the mind of the writer, he
cannot read Latin otherwise than slowly and painfully.
So, then, an absolutely essential thing to a man who
wants to read Latin is: —

4. A perfect working familiarity with the Roman
ways of constructing sentences.

Now we teach the first three things more or less
effectively, — vocabulary, inflection, syntax. Do we
teach the last?

I turn to the "First Latin Books," in order to find
what is said to students at that most critical period in
their study of the language, — the beginning. I re-
member well how I was taught at Phillips Exeter
Academy — of revered memory — to attack a Latin
sentence. " First find your verb, and translate it," said
my teacher. "Then find your subject, and translate
it. Then find the modifiers of the subject, then the
modifiers of the verb," etc., etc. Well, I had got more
than four years beyond Exeter before I learned to read
Latin with any feeling but that it was a singularly cir-
cuitous and perverted way of expressing ideas, which I
could not expect to grasp until I had reformed my
author's sentences and reduced them to English. Since
my time, however, better ways may have come into
vogue. So I turn to the books of two scholarly gen
tlemen of my acquaintance, — practical teachers, too,
— namely, Mr. Comstock, of Phillips Andover Academy, and Dr. Leighton, of the Brooklyn Latin School.
On page 233 of Mr. Comstock's " First Latin Book,"
and pages 211 and 212 of Dr. Leighton's " First Steps
in Latin," I find distinct rules, essentially the same, for

the operation in question.   The former begin as follows: —

(a.) In every simple sentence, find and translate

    (1) The subject.
    (2) The predicate.

Here is a new departure, an entire revolution since
my day.   I was taught to find first the *predicate*.   A
change so radical, a method so exactly the opposite of
the old one, ought to lead to results the opposite of the
old; namely, to the power to read Latin easily instead
of with difficulty.   So, with a cheerful heart, I take up
a simple sentence in the fourth oration against Catiline,
3, 5, and try my new method.

Haec omnia indices detulērunt.   I look for my subject.   Fortunately, it lies right at hand.   It is *haec*,
nom. pl.   Next I translate it, *these;* or, since it is neuter, *these things*.   Then I proceed to find the verb, which
again is obvious, viz., *detulerunt*, in 3d person pl., agreeing with the subject *haec*.   Perhaps I have caught from
somewhere the happy idea of not looking words up in
the dictionary until I have tried my hand at them.   So,
very properly, I set out with the simplest meaning I
can think of, viz., *brought*.   Now I am well started :
These things brought.   Next I look for the modifiers
of the subject, and find *omnia*.   I build it on, and have
now " *all these things* " for my subject, — " *all these things
brought*."   Next I look for the modifiers of the predicate, and I find *indices, witnesses*, acc. pl., object of
the verb.   Everything is straight.   *All these things
brought the witnesses*.   I pass on, and when I come to
the class-room, and the teacher calls on me, I read out,

"*All these things brought the witnesses*," prepared to parse it to the last word,—only to be told that I am entirely wrong.[1]

Now, a Roman boy of my age, and much less clever than I, if he could have smuggled himself into the senate that day, would have understood what those four words meant the instant Cicero uttered the last of them, *detulerunt*. What is the difference between us? Each of us, he and I, knew substantially the meaning of each word, each of us could inflect, each of us knew all the syntax required. Yet I missed the idea, while he got it. Wherein did he beat me? Why, simply here: I, following the direction of my teachers, first found my subject, and settled on *haec*. The Roman boy did not know whether *haec* was subject or object. He only knew it as *haec*. I knew that *detulerunt* was the verb, and so did he when it arrived. I knew that *omnia* agreed with the subject *haec*, while he only surmised that it *belonged* with *haec*, whatever that might prove to be. I knew that *indices* was the object, while he only felt that *indices* was subject *or* object, and that it was the opposite of *haec omnia* (apposition being out of the question), being object if that should turn out to be subject, and subject if that should turn out to be object. Then he heard *detulerunt*, and with that word everything dropped into place as simply as, in Milton's sentence following,

[1] If the example chosen is not a happy one, any teacher of young pupils — any college teacher even, I fear — could, with a few days' watching of a class, come upon examples that will satisfy him that the habitual method, no matter how high the teacher's aims, tends to bring about a laxity of scrutiny which constantly leads into blunders as bad as the instance here given.

> "... *the moon, whose orb*
> *Through optic glass the Tuscan artist views,*"

the last word resolves our momentary suspense in regard to the relation of orb and artist; which relation would have been precisely reversed, had we found such a word, *e.g.*, as *glads*.

Let us try the method further. Mr. Comstock goes on (the italics are in part my own) : —

b. In a Compound Sentence translate each principal clause as though it were a Simple Sentence. If there are Subordinate Clauses, translate them *in the order of their importance.* A Subordinate or Dependent Clause is one which, just as in English, limits some part of the Principal Clause (as described in 42, page 12). A clause introduced by a Latin word meaning *if, who, which, because, since, although, when, after, while,* etc., is Dependent, and *should be left* until the meaning of the Principal Clause has been obtained.

c. In a Complex Sentence, first translate the Principal Clause as a Simple Sentence ; then translate the Dependent Clauses according to directions given above (*b*).

But what *is* the order of their importance, and how am I to start? With the connective, I presume. We will suppose it to be *ut.* But how shall I translate it? There are some half-dozen or more "meanings": *in order to, so that, when, as, considering, although.* Which does it have here? I cannot tell. *No more could a Roman.* But the difference is, that a Roman did not *want* to tell which one of its forces *ut* had here, but waited until something in the rest of the sentence, perhaps twenty, perhaps fifty, words away, informed him ; while *I* am bidden, so to speak, to toss

up a cent, and start off upon a meaning, with the odds
heavily against me; possibly to find my mistake and go
back and correct it, more probably to add error on error
in order to "make sense," and so to get the whole thing
into a hopeless muddle.

Now, all this is wrong. It is a frightful source of
confusion to prowl about here and there in the sentence
in a self-blinded way that would seem pathetic to a
Roman, looking at things without the side-lights afford-
ed to him by the order; and, further, it is a frightful
waste of time. Take a sentence such as often occurs;
e.g., the opening of the third oration against Catiline,
delivered before the people. Imagine, now, two scenes:
on the one hand the Roman Forum, on Dec. 3, 63 B.C.,
with a mass of men and boys listening to Cicero as he
tells the story of the entangling of the conspirators re-
maining in Rome; on the other, a modern schoolroom,
say in the Syracuse High School (though I hope I am
about to slander Dr. Bacon), Dec. 3, 1886 A.D. In the
former case Cicero has the floor, as we say; in the
latter case, Dr. Bacon's assistant, book in hand, his
pupils before him. Both audiences want to get at the
same thing, — *what Cicero has to say*. In the first scene
Cicero proceeds : —

**Rem publicam, Quirites, vitamque omnium ves-
trum, bona, fortunas, coniuges liberosque vestros,
atque hoc domicilium clarissimi imperi, fortunatissimam pulcherrimamque urbem, hodierno die deorum
immortalium summo erga vos amore, laboribus consiliis periculis meis, e flamma atque ferro ac paene
ex faucibus fati ereptam et vobis conservatam ac
restitutam videtis.** → v. "You all have seen"

When he has said that, every soul that has heard him knows precisely what he means. Now change to the Syracuse High School. The teacher says, "first find your subject." So we run on, scenting out a subject : —

Rem publicam, Quirites, vitamque omnium vestrum, bona, fortunas, coniuges liberosque vestros, atque hoc domicilium clarissimi imperi, fortunatissimam pulcherrimamque urbem, hodierno die deorum immortalium summo erga vos amore, laboribus consiliis periculis meis, e flamma atque ferro ac paene ex faucibus fati ereptam et vobis conservatam ac restitutam videtis.

Well, we are through with the entire sentence, and there is no subject! Of course, then, it is implied in the verb, and is the 2d personal pronoun, in the plural. Next we find our verb. That is, as it happens, the last word, *videtis.* Then we go back, do we, and find the modifiers of the subject, and then the modifiers of the verb? *No,* I say to all that. *We have already,* if we have been rightly brought up, *understood everything in that sentence by the time we reach the last syllable of it, without having thought meanwhile of a single English word; and we are as ready in 1886 to go on immediately with the next sentence as we should have been if we had been Romans in the Roman Forum on that day in 63 B.C.* Or, to put it another way, the boy who, reaching that oration in the course of his preparation for college, cannot understand that particular sentence, and a great many much more difficult sentences in the oration, from reading it straight through once in the Latin, nay, *from merely hearing his teacher read it straight through once in the Latin*, has been wrongly trained, is wasting time sadly, out of a human life all too short, and, so far from being on the direct way to read Latin with speed and relish, and then to proceed to do so, is on the direct way to drop it just as soon as the elective system of his particular college will allow, and, if he cares for literature, to go into some language in which it is *not* necessary, first to find the subject, and then the predicate,. and then the modifiers of the subject, and then the modifiers of the predicate, and then to do the same thing for the subordinate sentence, or, if there are several subordinate sentences, to do the same thing for each one of them in the order of their importance, and then to put these tattered bits together into a patchwork.

Now, it will not do to say that students, by beginning in this way, get, quite early, beyond the need of it. At any rate, I can testify, from my own experience, that, in spite of the admirable efforts of the schools in "sight-reading," they do not, when they come to Harvard or Cornell. I allow myself in my class-room — keeping well inside of what is said to be customary among college professors — one jest a year. When I first meet the new Freshman class (for I could not bear to leave such precious material wholly to the most perfect assistant), I question them : "Suppose, now, you are set, as you were at the examination for admission the other day, to tell me the meaning of a sentence in a book you never saw, — say an oration of Cicero, — how do you proceed to get at the writer's meaning?" There is at once a chorus of voices (for they are crammed for that question, having learned printed directions, as we have seen, in the first books they studied), "*First find the* — SUBJECT," three-quarters of them say; "PRED‑ICATE," the other quarter. "Now here," I say to them, "is an unhappy difference of opinion about first princi‑ ples in a matter of everyday practice, and of very serious importance. Which is right?" They do not know. "Which do you suppose the Romans who heard the oration delivered in the Forum first hunted up, the subject or the predicate?" That little jest, simple as it is, always meets with great success; for it not only raises a laugh (of no value in itself), but it shows at once, even to a Freshman, the entire absurdity of try‑ ing to read Latin by a hunting-up first of either his subject or his predicate; and so enlists his sympathy in favor of trying some other way, if any can be shown him. But, at the same time, it proves to me that the method taught at the most critical of all periods, the beginning, is still wrong. Only in late years, and very rarely, does some student answer my question with: "First read the first Latin word without translating it, then the second, then the third, and so on to the end, taking in all the possible constructions of every word, while barring out at once the impossible, and, above all, erring, if anywhere, in the direction of keeping the mind in suspense unnecessarily long, waiting, at least, until a sure solution has been given by the sentence itself."

Yet this is the one method that should everywhere be rigorously used, from the day of the first lesson to the last piece of Latin that the college graduate reads to solace his old age. *Only, the process which at first is at every point conscious and slow*, as it was not with the Romans, *becomes, in Latin of ordinary difficulty, a process wholly unconscious and very rapid,* precisely as it was with the Romans. Just when the process would become easy for ordinarily simple Latin, if the training were right from the beginning, I cannot say. In my own experience with college students, all whose habits have to be changed, I find a striking difference to be produced in a single term. And at the end of two years, when the elective work begins, I now find it entirely practicable for the class to devote itself to the study of the Latin literature in the Latin alone, having nothing to do with version into English except at the examinations ; and I never had so good and so spirited translation, whether at sight or on the reading of the term, as last week, when, for the first time, I held such an examination at the end of a term spent without translation.

To bring the matter into a definite and practical shape, I can best indicate what it seems to me you ought to direct your teachers of Latin to do, *mutatis mutandis,* by telling you what I myself do from the time when I first meet my Freshmen to the end of the Sophomore year.

After my little jest about the Romans hunting up first the subject and then the predicate as Cicero talked to them, or first the predicate and then the subject, whichever one thinks the Roman method may have been, I assure them that "what we have to do is to learn to understand a Roman sentence precisely as a Roman understood it as he heard it or read it, say in an oration, for example. Now the Roman heard, or read, first the first word, then the second, then the third, and so on, through sentence after sentence, to the end of the oration, with no turning back, with no hunting around. And in doing this he was so guided all the time, by indications of one kind or another in some way strown through each sentence, that, when the last word of that sentence had been spoken or read, the whole of the meaning had reached his mind. The process of detecting these indications of meaning was to him a wholly unconscious one. We moderns, however, of course cannot begin so far along. What we are to reach finally is precisely this unconsciousness of processes; but we shall be obliged, for the first few years, explicitly to study the indications, until we come to know them familiarly, one after another. We must for some time think out, at every point, as the sentence progresses (and that without ever allowing ourselves to look ahead), all those conveyings of meaning, be they choice of word, or choice of order, or choice of case, or choice of mode, or choice of tense, or whatsoever else which at that point sufficed for the Roman mind. And when these indications — which after all are not so many in number — have come to be so familiar to us that most of them are ready to flash before the mind without our deliberately summoning them, we shall be very near the point at which, in Latin graded to our growing powers, we shall interpret indications unconsciously. And the moment we do that, we shall be reading Latin by the Roman's own method."

I take up now — all books being closed — a sentence of very simple structure, of which every word and every construction are familiar, say a certain passage in Livy.[1]

---

[1] I. 41.

I tell the story of the context: Two assassins have got admission, on the pretext of a quarrel to be decided, into the presence of Tarquin. One of them diverts the attention of the king by telling his tale, and the other brings down an axe upon the king's head; whereupon they both rush for the door.

In order that the interpretation shall be done absolutely in the order in which a Roman would do it, without looking ahead, I write one word at a time upon the board (as I will again do upon the board before you), and ask questions as I go, as follows [1] : —

Tarquinium. "What did Livy mean by putting that word at the beginning of the sentence?" *That the person mentioned in it is at this point of conspicuous importance.* "Where is **Tarquinium** made?" *In the accusative singular.* "What does that fact mean to your minds?"

Here most of them are somewhat dazed, not being used to that word *meaning*, the very word that ought constantly to be used in dealing with syntax, or so-called "parsing." So I very probably have to say, "May it mean the duration of time of the act with which it is connected?" They say, *No.* I ask, "Why not?" Somebody says, *Because the name of a person cannot indicate time.* I say, "Give me some words that *might* indicate time." They give me *dies, noctes, aetatem,* etc. Then I ask, "May it mean extent of space?" They say, *No,* give me similar reasons for their answer, and,

---

[1] The sentence grows upon the board by the addition of one word after another. To obtain the same result in print, with each new word the whole of the sentence thus far given will be repeated. And, for the sake of greater clearness, answers will be distinguished from questions by the use of italics.

upon my asking for words that *might* indicate extent of space, they give me, perhaps, *mille passuum, tres pedes*, etc. Then I ask, "May it indicate the extent of the action of the verb, the degree to which the action goes?" They say, *No*, for a similar reason. But when I ask for words that *might* mean the degree of the action, they commonly cannot tell me, for the reason that, strange to say, the grammars do not recognize such a usage; though sentences like *he walks a great deal every day (multum cottidie ambulat)* are even more common than sentences like *he walks three miles every day (cottidie tria milia passuum ambulat)*, and the accusatives mean essentially the same thing in both sentences. Then I ask, "May it mean that in respect to which something is said, — *as regards Tarquin*, — the accusative of specification?" To a question like that, I am sorry to say that a great many always answer *yes*, for students get very vague notions of the real uses of the Latin accusative of specification. Somebody, however, may be able to tell me that the name of a person is never used in the accusative of specification, and that in general the use of the accusative of specification, in the days of Cicero and Virgil, was mostly confined to poetry. "What words *were used* in the accusative of specification in prose?" Here I never get an answer, although the list is determinate, short, and important. So I have to say, "I must add to your working knowledge a useful item; write in your note-books as follows: *partem, vicem, genus* with *omne* or a pronoun (*quod, hoc, id*), *secus* with *virile* or *muliebre, hoc* and *id* with *aetatis*, the relative *quod* and the interrogative *quid*, are used in Latin prose in all periods as accusatives of

Partem = portion, part (AU.)   Vicem = change; interaction;
    genus = race   function.
    labtimeicero

specification. Here, then, is a bit of definite information which may enable you, when you first meet one of
these words again (you will do so quite early in your
first book of Livy), to walk without stumbling through
a sentence where you would otherwise trip." Then I
go back to **Tarquinium.** "May it be," I ask, "an
accusative of exclamation?" They say, *Possibly so.*
I say, "possibly yes, though in historical narration you
would hardly expect such an exclamation from the his-
torian." Next I ask, "May it be a cognate accusative?" To that they answer, *No;* telling me, perhaps
with some help, that *the name of a person cannot be
in any sense a restatement of an act, — cannot mean an
activity.* "Well, then, what *does* this accusative case
mean?" By this time a good many are ready to say:
Object of a verb, or in apposition with the object. But
I ask if one thing more is possible, and some one says:
Subject of an infinitive. "Yes," I answer; "and one
thing more yet?" *Predicate of an infinitive,* some
one suggests.

"Now," I ask, "what have we learned from all this?
Given the name of a person or persons in the accusative
with no preposition, how many and what constructions
are possible?" All are ready now to answer, *Object of
a verb, or subject or predicate of an infinitive.* "Good,"
I say. "Keep those possibilities always fresh in your
mind, letting them flash through it the moment you
see such a word; and, that having been done, WAIT, and
NEVER DECIDE which of these possible meanings was in
the mind of the Roman speaker or writer until the rest
of the sentence has made the answer to that question
perfectly clear. Now tell me what constructions are

possible for an accusative like *hiemem.*" They answer, *duration of time, apposition, object of verb, subject or predicate of an infinitive.* "For an accusative like *pedes?*" They answer, *extent of space, apposition, object of verb, or subject or predicate of an infinitive.* "For an accusative like *multum?*" *Extent of action, apposition, object of verb, or subject or predicate of an infinitive.* "For an accusative like *vitam?*" *Cognate accusative, apposition, object of verb, or subject or predicate of an infinitive.* Now I ask, "Can any one tell me what constructions we may expect if the verb turns out to be some word like *doceo* or *celo?*" They all give the answer, and therewith I have already passed in rapid review practically the whole matter of the accusative constructions; and, what is more, — and this is vital, — I have done it *from a very practical stand-point.* I have not asked a student to "parse" a word *after seeing its full connection in the sentence* (an exercise which loses four-fifths of its virtue by this misplacement), but I have demanded *anticipatory parsing,* — I have put my questions in such a way that my students have learned for all accusatives what instantaneous suggestions of the possible parts a word is playing in the sentence they may get, at first sight of the word, from the very nature of the word. Then I pass on. We have our King Tarquin before our eyes, as the person on whom the interest of the sentence centres, and we know that he is the object of an action, or the subject or predicate of an infinitive action ; or, possibly, in apposition with such an object, subject, or predicate. To proceed, the next word, **moribundum,** is what and where made?" *Adjective, nom. sing. neut., or acc. sing. masc.*

or neut. Don't smile at all this. The habit of getting
a young student to think all these things out, even where
he could not go astray if they were not asked of him,
saves many a getting lost in difficult places. "What is
probable about *moribundum,* as we have it in this
particular sentence?" *That it belongs to Tarquinium.*
"Right. Now keep that picture in mind : **Tarquinium
moribundum, the King, breathing his last, acted
upon or acting.** Now for the next word : **Tarquinium
moribundum cum.** What is **cum**?" Some say, with
perfect readiness, *preposition,* some say *conjunction.*[1]
"But," I answer, "if you are used to the right spell-
ing, you know with an instant's thought that no Roman
that ever lived could tell at this point whether it was
preposition or conjunction. In order to tell, you must
wait for — what?" *Ablative or verb,* they answer.
Then we go on, "**Tarquinium moribundum cum qui.**
What does **qui** at once tell us about **cum**?" *Conjunction.* "Right. What do we now know, with almost
absolute certainty, about *Tarquinium?* What part of
the sentence does it belong to?" Here, I grieve to say,
a chorus of voices always answers, *Main verb;* for, in
some mysterious way, students arrive at the universities
without having learned that the Romans delighted to
take out the most important word, or combination of
words, from a subordinate introductory sentence, and

---

[1] The fact that it is possible for students, without a moment's reflec-
tion, to plunge at things in this sadly well-known way shows how
thoroughly ineffective the prevailing method of teaching beginners is
in developing a sharp and self-suspicious observation. That charge,
it will be seen, cannot be brought against the method advocated in this
paper.

put it at the very start, before the connective, — a bit
of information worth a great deal for practical reading.
That habit of expression I now tell them, and then ask,
" Given a sentence beginning with *mors si*, what do
you know ? " *That mors is the subject or predicate of
the verb introduced by si.* " Given a sentence introduced by *Hannibali victori cum ceteri ?* " *That Hannibali depends on something in the cum-sentence.* Now we
go back to our sentence, and the word **qui**. What part
of speech is it ? " *Relative*, they say. " Or what else ? "
I ask. *Interrogative.* " Where is it made ? " *Nom.,
sing. or plur., masc.* " If it is a relative, where in the
sentence as a whole does its antecedent lie ? " They
should answer, *Inside the cum-clause.* The *cum* serves
as the first of two brackets to include the *qui*-clause.
" If, on the other hand, it is an interrogative, what kind
of a question is alone here possible ? " *Indirect, and in
the subjunctive*, they answer. " In that case, what kind
of a meaning, speaking generally, must the verb introduced by *cum* have ? " *It must be able to imply asking
of some kind.* " Rightly said; perhaps we may have
such a sentence as, *When everybody inquired who these
men were — Cum qui essent omnes quaererent;* or perhaps
we shall find that **qui** is relative. The next word is
circa, — Tarquinium moribundum cum qui circa.
What part of speech is it ? " *Adverb.* " What then may
it do ? " *It may modify a verb, an adjective, or another
adverb.* We proceed: **Tarquinium moribundum cum
qui circa erant.** " What, now, about **circa** ? " *It
modifies* **erant**. " What was the number of **qui** ? "
Plural. " Was it relative or interrogative ? " *Relative.*
" How do you know ? " *Because* **erant** *is not subjunc-*

tive. "Right. Now **qui circa erant** is as good as a noun or a pronoun, — an indeclinable noun or pronoun, in the plural. Think of it in that way, as we go on. **Tarquinium moribundum cum qui circa erant excepissent.** I don't ask to-day the meaning of the mode of **excepissent,** because the world is in so much doubt about the question of the history and force of the *cum*-constructions. But what *was* Livy's meaning in writing the accusative **Tarquinium?**" *Object of* **excepissent.** "Yes, and what was the subject of **excepissent?**" *The antecedent of* **qui.** "Yes; or, looking at the matter more generally, the subject was **qui circa erant.**"

"Before going on what picture have we before us? What has the sentence thus far said? This : **See Tar-quin, dying! See the bystanders! See them pick him up!** Our curiosity is stimulated by the very order. The next word is **illos,** — **Tarquinium moribundum cum qui circa erant excepissent** . . . What does the position of **illos,** first in the main sentence proper, tell us?" *That the people meant by it are of special prominence at this point.* "Who do you suppose these **illos** are, these *more distant persons,* thus set in emphatic balance against **Tarquinium,** each leading its clause?" *The assassins,* the whole class say. "What do we know about Livy's meaning from the case?" Now they all answer in fine chorus and completeness, *Apposition, object of main verb, or subject or predicate of infinitive.* We proceed: **Tarquinium moribundum cum qui circa erant excepissent, illos fugientes** . . . "What part of speech is **fugientes?**" *Participle.* "Which one?" *Present active.* "Then you see a running-away going on before your eyes. What gender?" *Masc. or fem.*

"What number?" *Plural.* "Then you see some two or more men or women running away. What case?" *Nom. or. acc.* "On the whole, do you feel sure you know the case?" *Yes; accusative.* "Belonging to what?" **Illos.** "Why?" *Because of course the assassins, the* **illos,** *would run away.* "Yes," I say; "but it cannot possibly mislead you to wait until there isn't a shadow of a doubt. We will go on: **Tarquinium moribundum cum qui circa erant excepissent, illos fugientes lictores . . .** Here you have another set of people, the king's body-guard. In what case?" *Nom. or acc. plural.* "Which?" They do not know. "Well, then, can **illos** agree with **lictores,** if you consider forms alone?" *Yes.* "In that case, **fugientes** would have to go with **illos lictores,** wouldn't it?" *Yes.* "But would the lictors run away?" *No.* "Would the assassins?" *Yes.* "Certainly. Then **fugientes** does not belong with **lictores,** and *does* belong with **illos**; and **illos** seems to be, just as we suspected at first sight of it, the *assassins.* However, we must ask ourselves one more question, Is *apposition* possible between **illos** and **lictores?**" *No; for they are very different people.* "Is any relation of a *predicate* possible between them? Can the one be the predicate of an infinitive of which the other is the subject?" *No; because, as before, they are very different people.* "Still it is possible that **lictores** is accusative. If it is, it may be object, in which case **illos** is necessarily subject, for, as we have seen, they cannot be in apposition; or, it may be subject, in which case, for the same reason, **illos** must be object. In either case, they must be in *direct opposition* to each other, one of them (we don't yet know which) being subject, the

other, object; while, if **lictores** is nom., you still have
the same relation, only you know which is subject and
which is object.   In any event, you see they are set
over against each other, together making subject and
object.   Now keep the results of this reasoning ready
for the countless cases in which such combinations
occur.   Given two nouns like **bellum Saguntum**: what
are the constructions?"   *One is the subject of a verb,
and the other the object, and we can't yet tell which.*
"Right.   Now I will give you a still more involved
combination, but of a very commonly occurring kind, —
quae nos materiem. What do you make out of that?"
Some clever boy will say, *Nos must be the subject of a verb,
either finite or infinitive, and quae and materiem are object and predicate-object.*   "Good.   Then what kind of
meaning does the verb probably have?"   *One of calling.*   "Right.   The words are from Lucretius, and the
verb he used was **vocamus**. Treasure up that combination, and the meaning of it."

  "Now we go back to the assassins who are running
away, and the king's body-guard.   I will inform you
that there is just one more word in the sentence. What
part of speech is it?"   *Verb.*   "Active or passive?
Active.   "Right.   What does it tell?"   *Tells what the
lictors do to the assassins.*   "What mode, then?"   *Indicative.*   "What two tenses are possible?"   *The perfect
and the historical present.*   "Right.   Now the situation is a pretty dramatic one.   Which of these two tenses
should you accordingly choose, if you were writing the
story?"   *The present.*   "So did Livy.   Now tell me
what you think the verb is."   *Interficiunt,* somebody
says.   *Capiunt,* says another, hitting the idea but not

the right word, which is **comprehendunt**, *get hold of them well,* — *nab 'em ;* or, as our tamer English phrase might put it, *secure them.*"

"Now let us render into English the sentence as a whole, translating not merely Livy's words, but the actual development of the thought in his mind. **Tarquinium**, *there's Tarquin ;* **moribundum**, *he's a dying man ;* **cum qui circa erant**, *you see the bystanders about to do something ;* **excepissent**, *they have caught and supported the king ;* **illos**, *you turn and look at the assassins ;* **fugientes**, *they are off on the run ;* **lictores**, *there are the king's body-guard ; we hold our breath in suspense ;* — **comprehendunt**, THEY'VE GOT 'EM ! So, then, that Latin order, which looks so perverted to one who is trained to pick the sentence to pieces and then patch it together again, gives us the very succession in which one would see the actual events; weaves all the occurrences together into a compact whole, yet keeping everywhere the *natural* order; while any order that we may be able to invent for a corresponding *single sentence* in English will twist and warp the natural order into a shape that would greatly astonish a Roman."

"Finally, with the understanding and sense of the dramatic in the situation, which we have got by working the sentence out as Livy wrote it, compare the perversion of it which we get by working it out correctly on the first-find-your-subject-of-the-main-sentence-and-then-your-predicate, etc., method: **the lictors secure the assassins as they run away, when those who were standing by had caught and supported the dying Tarquin.** The facts are all there, but the *style*, the *soul*, is gone."

Then I at once bring what we have learned to bear by giving a piece of blank paper to each student and starting out upon a new sentence, which shall involve what we have just seen, together with some fresh matter. The questions are carefully studied and written out in advance, and the place of each is indicated to me, in my prepared manuscript, by a number attached to the Latin word concerned, as if for a foot-note. As each question is put, the number is at once written down by each student, and his answer written out. Afterwards my assistant carefully goes through every paper, and with a colored pencil marks every error, for my own guidance, and for the subsequent study, penitence, and profit of the writer. The following is an example actually used, from Livy, 21, 53. The answer that should be written is given with each question.

Hannibal[1] cum[2] quid[3 4 5 6 7 8 9] optimum[10 11 12] foret[13] hosti[14] cerneret,[15 16] vix[17] ullam spem[18 19] habebat[20] temere[21 22] atque[23 24] ____[25] ____[26] consules[27 28 29 30 31] ____[32].

1. Construction?
   Subject of a verb, either subordinate or main.
2. Part of speech?
   Preposition or conjunction.
3. **Cum** was what part of speech?
   Conjunction.
4. Construction of **Hannibal**?
   Subject or predicate nominative of verb introduced by **cum**.
5. **Quid** is what part of speech?
   Interrogative.
6. Construction of the verb to which **quid** belongs?
   Subjunctive of indirect question.
7. General nature of meaning of verb introduced by **cum**?
   Some meaning that can imply a question.

8. Case of **quid**?
   Nom. or acc. neut. sing.
9. Construction of **quid**?
   Subject, predicate, or object of finite verb or infinitive; or
   acc. of specification, the so-called adverb.
10. Case?
    Nom. neut. sing., or acc. masc. or neut. sing.
11. Construction?
    If neut., agreeing with subject or object of verb, or in
    predicate. If masc., agreeing with object of verb, or
    with subject or predicate of an infinitive.
12. What constructions may follow to complete the meaning of
    optimum?
    Dat. of the person for whom something is **optimum**, or abl.
    of that with respect to which something is **optimum**. (It
    is worth while to have those two possibilities pat, for the
    great class of words of which **optimum** is a specimen.)
13. Where made?
    Imperfect subjunctive. (Reason already given under 6.)
14. Construction?
    Dative after **optimum**. (Reason given under 12.)
15. Where made, and introduced by what?
    Imperfect subjunctive, introduced by **cum**.
16. Construction of **Hannibal**?
    Subject of **cerneret**.
17. **Vix**, *hardly*, has a negative feeling. In such a connection,
    what would be the pronoun meaning *any*, and what the
    adjective? (Probably nobody knows.)
    Quisquam, ullus.
18. Construction?
    Acc. sing., object of verb, or subject or predicate of infinitive.
19. **Spes**, just as much as **spero**, indicates a mental activity,
    and we shall probably find something else completing its
    meaning, the *object* of the **spes**. What will be the case
    (*a*) if the completing word is a noun?
    Objective genitive.
    (*b*) If the completing word is a verb?
    Objective genitive of gerund or of gerundive with noun, or
    future infinitive.

20. Subject is what?
    A pronoun, repeating **Hannibal.**
21. Part of speech, and simplest meaning?
    Adverb, meaning *blindly.*
22. Bearing in mind that, in the ordinary Roman habit, words
    were placed in *anticipation* of those which they modify,
    not after them, what do you feel about **temere**?
    That it modifies the expected object of **spem**, which, conse-
    quently, is a verb.
23. Probably introduces what?
    Another adverb, corresponding to **temere**.
24. Write an adverb to mean *not looking ahead.*
    Improvide.
25. Write nom. or acc. neut. sing. meaning *anything* (in one word).
    Quicquam.
26. In what case is that word here, and with what verb is it con-
    nected?
    Acc., connected with a verb, which verb must depend on **spem**.
27. Where made, without reference to context?
    Nom. or acc. plur.
28. Where made, with reference to context? and how do you know?
    Acc., because **habebat** is sing.
29. Meaning of this accusative?
    That **consules** is subject, object, or predicate of an infinitive.
30. Relation of **quicquam** and **consules** to each other?
    One the object, the other the subject, of the infinitive.
31. Complete the sentence, using a verb meaning *do.*
    Acturos, with or without **esse.**
32. Write, in the best English you have at your command, a
    translation of the sentence.

"Now," I go on to say to my students, "you are to
commit this sentence to memory, and be ready to give
it fluently in the Latin when we meet next. And in
the same way you will commit to memory every passage we so use in the year; and at each term examination you will find yourselves called upon to write one

of these passages, still from memory. Further, and still more important than this, never again pick out your subject, your predicate, etc.; but, in preparing your daily lessons, do just what we have been doing this morning, except that you are not to translate. any sentence, or any part of any sentence, until you have gone through the whole lesson in the Latin, and got all the meaning in your power out of it. I give you a short lesson, and I shall call upon one man and another to take up a sentence and go rapidly through it as Latin, word after word, as we have just now done, telling us precisely how it should be thought out. In preparing your lesson, in order to be sure that your eye does not stray and run ahead, cut out a piece of flexible pasteboard, or, until you can get pasteboard, a piece of stiff writing-paper, as long as twice the width of your printed text, and two or three inches wide. Cut a strip from the top, running along half the length, and deep enough to correspond to precisely one line of your text, including the space that belongs with it.[1] Use this piece of

[1] At the meeting of the Philological Association at Ithaca last summer, Professor Gildersleeve, in the course of some remarks upon the reading of Greek and Latin, expressed himself with great severity in regard to the habitual way of doing the thing, and suggested that it would be desirable, in order to force students to accept the order of the original, to require them to read through a hole in a piece of paper, or with a notched card. The method urged in the present pamphlet is practically so entirely identical with the results that would flow from Professor Gildersleeve's suggestion, that nothing but the fact that this method was already substantially in print in the Cornell University Register for 1885–6, and in the special announcement of courses in the classics, could save this pamphlet from the suspicion of being merely an expansion of Professor Gildersleeve's hint. The same thing holds in regard to the admirable injunction in the preface to the new

paper in such a way as to expose just one word at a time, together with which, of course, will also be seen all the words preceding; that is to say, as you think about one word after another, pushing your paper on, you will constantly see all of the sentence thus far traversed, without being able to look ahead."

At the next meeting, the class, thus prepared, recites as described, a number of students attempting to show precisely what mental processes one should go through in taking up the sentences of the lesson. At the next but one, and thereafter throughout the Freshman year, all books being closed, the instructor reads the review lesson aloud, with all the effectiveness possible to him, one sentence at a time, calling for a translation of it from one and another student.[1] As a preparation for this exercise, each student is urged to read the review aloud a number of times in his own room, doing his author as much justice as possible.

At every exercise during the year, except the special weekly exercise, a number of sentences, prepared by the instructor, and based upon the text under reading at the time, are given out to students, to be written upon the board, in the English and in Latin, while the rest of the class are engaged upon translating the review as the instructor reads it; and when the work

edition of the Allen and Greenough Cicero, published in May, 1886. As it is, however, it appears that the essential aim of the method of this pamphlet (not necessarily, of course, its details) has strong and express confirmation.

[1] For this very helpful feature of the work under description, I owe my thanks to my assistant, Dr. A. C. White. I know of no piece of work more charming and cheering to listen to, excepting the translating of a new piece of Latin in the same way.

upon the review is over, these Latin sentences upon the board are criticised by the class. I touch upon a very serious defect in most of our preparatory schools when I say that from beginning to end there should never be a recitation in a foreign language without written or oral translation into that language.

For the special weekly exercise described above, there can be no considerable preparation beyond incessant faithfulness in the daily work. The time thus left free is utilized in the preparation of a formal written translation of a considerable piece of English based upon the Latin recently read. (It will be seen that no textbook in composition is employed.) The exercise handed in by each student is afterwards looked through, and returned to him at the next meeting of the class, with all errors marked.

The writing of the Latin sentence, one word at a time, upon the board in the special weekly exercise which has been described above, gives place in a few weeks to the corresponding dictation of one word at a time, to be written upon his paper by the student, the questions being, of course, given as before. The exercise changes constantly in character by the dropping of questions with which the students have become familiar, and the bringing in of questions involving new principles. Meanwhile, the examination of the papers written shows, from week to week, just where each student's weakness lies. In no long time all the constantly recurring constructions have become familiar as practical, working affairs. Then (and this time properly comes somewhere near the end of the first third of the year) I cease entirely to have the Latin written, and give my passage (which may now be of respectable length) orally, still asking occasional questions for written answers, here and there, at points dangerous or otherwise instructive. After the whole of the passage has been gone through with in this way, it is taken up again, one sentence at a time, and a written translation is made by each student. The passages are commonly selected from the book which the class is reading, and not very far in advance of the place reached in the other lessons of the week. The attempt is always made to select a passage with a dramatic or otherwise striking close. Each week, as already said, the whole of the exercise of the previous week is memorized, and repeated by several students, with great attention to the effective conveying of the meaning, by the throwing together, as in all spoken languages, of a number of words making a group in the sentence as a whole, by the careful balancing, in the delivery, of words clearly meant to be balanced, etc., etc. All this time each student is gaining a working knowledge of syntax regarded from the true standpoint for the first purposes of college work, namely, as a mechanism for conveying meaning from one mind to another; is learning to bring that knowledge of syntax to bear at the most economical point; is gaining familiarity with Roman tricks of order; and is laying up a steadily growing vocabulary.[1] And throughout, in order to keep constantly in sight the idea that the aim of the whole business is to learn to

[1] To vary the exercise, a continuous story of several pages in length is occasionally read through without stopping and without repetition, and each student then writes as complete a résumé of it as he can produce.

read Latin, occasional examinations in translating new passages from a text or printed paper are held during the term (as of course they should be upon any system), and at the end of each term the first exercise at the final examination is translation at hearing, the second exercise is translation at sight, the third exercise is translation at sight from English into Latin, the fourth is the writing of one of the passages memorized during the term; and not until this is done does the student proceed to an exercise in translating and commenting upon passages read during the term. Moreover, the greater part of the grammatical questions of the paper are set, not upon passages read during the term, but upon the passages given for the first time at the examinations; namely, the passages to be translated at hearing and at sight.

In the second year, the aim of gaining in power to read at sight is constantly held up before the students, and occasional written examinations in reading at sight are given through the term, while the first exercise set at the examination at the end of the term is always translation at sight. A proper supplement to this is an elective in the speaking and writing of Latin. In the second and third terms of the second year, which are now devoted to Horace, considerable quantities can be read, with a good deal of memorizing; and the treatment can be made almost wholly literary. That carries us through the Sophomore year, and to the beginning of the elective work, taken by Juniors and Seniors together. Here translation at the daily lesson ends, except in those rare cases where the meaning of a difficult passage cannot be given by explaining the grammatical structure, or by turning the passage into some other form in Latin.[1] Translations are written at occasional exercises held for that purpose during the term, and always make a part of the final examination, so that every student feels bound to understand his author. But the students are urged not to have anything to do with English in preparation for their daily lessons or for the final examination, but to prepare to read the Latin *as literature*, with the utmost skill in rendering their author that they can acquire.

In all my teaching, two exercises stand out from the rest, as giving me special delight through the interest and mental activity of my students: first, the exercises with the Freshmen, which I have described as carried on weekly by myself; secondly, an exercise such as I carried on with an elective class recently, when, at the end of a term spent upon Plautus, I read a new play straight through in the Latin (the students follow-

[1] The preparation indicated has been leading for some years toward the dropping of translation at the daily recitations, and, indeed, I have always endeavored to secure time toward the end of the hour in which to read on in advance to my students, without translating. But I should not have had the courage in the present year to break with translation in the class-room in advanced reading, had it not been for the assurances given me by Professor Greenough, founded upon his own experiments in doing this precise thing. My experience in the past term has been so gratifying as to lead me to desire greatly that Professor Greenough might set forth, in accessible form, the great advantages of the system for students properly trained for it. Meanwhile, let me premise that the delight of this method of dealing with a literature — the charm of direct communication with the author, of feeling, in fact, the very untranslatableness of diction and style — cannot be fancied by one who has not made the experiment; always supposing, of course, that the class has been trained in advance and brought to the point at which such reading is made possible.

ing me in their texts), without translation, and with
very little comment, moving at about the rate at which
one would move if he were reading a new play of
Shakespeare in a similar way; and felt my audience
responsive, even to the extent of occasional laughter
that checked us for a moment, to nearly everything in
our author that would have been intelligible, without
special explanation, in an English translation.

Finally, if you ask me whether this method which
I have been describing does not take a great deal of
time, I shall answer that the amount of Latin read in
the first term is much smaller than in the ordinary
way, but that the power to read increases rapidly, and
that the tõtal quantity read in the first year is somewhat greater than on the common system, considerably
greater in the second year, and in the elective years
altogether greater; to say nothing of the much juster
understanding of, and more intimate feeling for, his
original, and the much keener delight in reading, gained
by the student who pursues this method. But there
is one thing more to be said about this kind of work,
this training of the student to read Latin rapidly. *It
is not the work of the universities at all.* In the universities, men should not learn how to read Latin, but
should read it. It should be my office, for instance, to
make them acquainted with the body of the literature,
to make them know it, at any rate, and love it, if possible. But the office of preparing them to do this by
training them to read ordinary Latin with ease and
speed belongs to no college instructor, but to the schools
of which you have charge. I wholly believe that the
application, from the very first day of reading a Roman

sentence of one word, of the method here described, would, without adding a day to the length of time given to preparation for college, make a young student able, at the beginning of his Freshman year, to read Latin with more ease and speed than are my students at the end of it,— to say nothing of the greater pleasure which they would have in their work. And I am not judging from my experience in university teaching alone; for this very method of teaching has been used by students of my own upon young pupils, of varying ability, in preparation for college, and with results that fully confirm my belief. Nor are the young pupils the only gainers. The teacher himself will be surprised to see how much more pleasure he feels in his work; and, if he keeps up his reading of the Latin literature, as all teachers of course endeavor to do, he will be surprised to find how his rate of speed will increase. And the method itself will give him no trouble to learn; for in the very act of preparing papers for examinations of this sort, or, at the worst, of conducting oral exercises without preparation, the teacher will very soon have taught himself the whole art.

SUPPLEMENT.

To the preceding address — long, and yet too brief — I wish to add two things : further specimens of papers actually employed by myself with a Freshman class, and suggestions for the application of the method in the preparatory schools.

At this point, I should advise the wearied reader, if he feels some confidence in the method, to lay the pamphlet aside and make experiment himself with a class, returning to the reading after he has come to feel an interest in further suggestions of detail. As for the wearied reader that does not feel this confidence, he will readily lay the pamphlet down unadvised.

SPECIMENS OF PAPERS.

In giving in this way details of the system on which my own work is conducted, I do not feel that I owe an apology. One who proposes a method must have a very solid basis for his proposal. This basis must be an experience of the efficacy of that which he is urging; and this experience should be given with the greatest clearness and definiteness. It is to be wished, indeed, that teachers of a given subject throughout the country, in colleges and schools, might regard themselves as forming one body with a common purpose, and that a constant interchange of experience and opinion might go on among them, alike in matters of investigation and matters of pedagogy.

It should be remembered that the papers printed below were used, early in the Freshman year, with students who had prepared for college upon the familiar and thoroughly un-Roman system. If students were prepared upon the right method, not one in ten of the questions here indicated would need to be asked, and the exercise of translating at hearing would be a rapid and attractive affair.

These papers were given to the Freshman class in succession, at intervals of a week, in the autumn of 1885; at which time the work of the other recitations of the week was in Livy. The constant aim — and the class were so informed — was to find for these papers, as given week after week, passages which would demand of them a practical power of handling constructions which had been discussed in the other exercises of the week, so that their progress should be one of constant acquisition without loss; and it was promised them that in this way they should in a short time possess a ready and *available* familiarity with all the commonly recurring constructions of the language. I further told them that, since I should not give them at these exercises in translation the meaning of any word which they had ever seen before, they had a very strong reason for laying up for themselves a vocabulary through securing in their memory every Latin word occurring in their daily work, and a very strong reason for paying extremely careful attention, both at and after the other recitations of the week, to any explanations of meaning of this or that word, alone, or in connection with others related to it in meaning (*e.g.*, to *alius*, in connection with *alter* and *ceteri*), which might similarly be given to them at the ordinary recitations. Nor was I content with this; for, in order that there might be no escape, I prepared a partial syllabus of definable points emphasized in the work of the term; and one of these was purchased, from the office that printed it, by each student in the class.

At the beginning of the term, the work of the advance lesson was largely done in the class-room, instructor and instructed working together. It will be rightly inferred from this that the class moved slowly at the outset. I am a devout believer in the reading of large quantities of the classics; indeed, that is, in this present business, my particular and precise aim; but I am also a believer in what is called "the long run," and "in the long run" only a soundly trained man gets very far. In the preliminary training, it is necessary at first to take a good deal of time in probing to the quick, sometimes with considerable distress to the would-be athletes, a class of new students who have been carefully trained to distort and mangle the Latin sentence; who have necessarily failed to acquire the alert and self-watchful habits of thought and of suspended judgment to which the received method, with its resulting impatience to "make sense," is practically strongly opposed; whose knowledge of syntax is of a back-handed kind, good for very little except to "parse" with, more or less mechanically and ineffectually, after the whole sentence has been dug out, but worth nothing as yet for the current interpretation of the syntax of word after word *in situ* in the progress of the sentence; and, finally, some of whom have been trained to pronounce Latin on the English method, others on the Continental.

and others on one or another of that great variety of
methods passing current under the general appellation
of " Roman," and many of whom, accordingly, find it
very difficult to understand a word of one syllable as
pronounced by my assistant or myself, — to say nothing
of a word of two syllables.

Up to the fourth week inclusive, the Latin was written upon the board at these weekly' exercises, one word
at a time, the questions being put, as indicated by the
footnotes in the papers given below, at one point and
another as the sentence progressed. For several weeks
after that time, the Latin sentence was written by each
student, one word at a time, as pronounced by the instructor, the questions being set and answered as before.
After this, the writing of the Latin was forbidden, and
the passages used were interpreted only as *heard* from
the instructor's reading.

At the first interview, the class had worked out, as it
was put upon the board, one word at a time, the sentence in Liv. I. 1, 5.

**Ibi egressi Troiani, ut quibus ab immenso prope
errore nihil praeter arma et naves superesset, cum
praedam ex agris agerent, Latinus rex Aborigines-
que, qui tum ea tenebant loca, ad arcendam vim
advenarum armati ex urbe atque agris concurrunt.**

As we reached the point ... *ut quibus*, they had made
out, under questioning, that *ut* might be (1) a conjunction, in which case *quibus* could be (*a*) an interrogative
introducing an indirect question depending on the *ut-*
verb, or (*b*) a relative referring to something connected
with the *ut*-verb; or that, on the other hand, *ut* might
be (2) an adverb, in which case the *quibus*-clause must

be substantially an adjective modifying *Troiani;* in other words, a *characterizing* clause. In this connection they had been told, for the sake of having the whole matter secured for their repertory of combinations of this kind, that what was essential in this latter case was the characterizing clause itself, and that in strictness no introductory word was necessary; if one were used, however, it might be either *ut, utpote,* or *quippe;* and it was also pointed out that, while there were three possibilities for a combination like *ut quibus,* there was only one possibility for a combination like *utpote quibus* or *quippe quibus.*

As we reached *superesset,* it was pointed out, against the practical habit of thought of nearly all the class, that, since in Latin the common practice was to put a modifying clause or phrase *before* the thing modified, the chances were that the *quibus*-clause, if it should turn out to be a characterizing clause, would bear, not upon *egressi,* but upon something which we were still to wait for. (This something turned out to be *cum . . . agerent,* — *the natural thing for destitute men to do.*)

As we reached . . . *cum praedam,* at which stage it was sure that *cum* was a conjunction, the point was made, though again against the sentiments of the class, that *Troiani* was the subject of the verb introduced by *cum,* since the Romans were fond of taking out a conspicuous word or phrase belonging to an introductory temporal sentence, and putting it *before* the connective.[1]

---

[1] It must already be apparent that I do not regard the "Sauveur method" as sufficient in dealing with a language so difficult as the Latin, and in a community where no amount of exertion will make Latin the habitual medium of daily speech. But I feel, nevertheless,

The passage chosen for the first written exercise turned out to be a little too difficult in the reasoning at the *et cui* point, though it had a certain and considerable usefulness in displaying to the class a sentence of which some of them, though knowing the meaning of each word, and though able to "parse" it from beginning to end if it were once translated to them, would yet fail to comprehend the meaning, through a lack of a *working* knowledge of the constructions involved.

‵ FIRST EXERCISE (Livy I. 34, 7).

[Tanaquil has been urging upon Lucumo, who lives in Tarquinii, that he would have better hopes of rising in some new city, and points out that Rome has special advantages.]

Facile[1] persuadet[2][3] ut[4][5] cupido[6][7] honorum et[8][9] cui[10][11] Tarquinii[12] materna[13][14] tantum[15][16] patria[17][18][19] ——; sublatis[20] itaque rebus[21][22] commigrant[23] ——[24].

1. May be either of what possible parts of speech; and where made?
   Adj. in nom. or acc. neut. sing.; or adverb.
2. In what way will the person who is persuaded, if there is one, be expressed?
   By the dative.
3. In what way will that to which the person is persuaded be expressed, if it proves to be (*a*) a pronoun?
                          (*b*) a verbal idea?
   (*a*) By the accusative.
   (*b*) By the infinitive, if it is a statement of belief, etc.; by a substantive purpose clause, if it be an act desired to be brought about.
4. The suspense about **facile** is now probably how resolved?
   The writer meant it as adverb, modifying **persuadet**.

that we owe a great debt of gratitude to Dr. Sauveur and his followers for their insistance that the language shall be treated as living, and as intelligible to the ear.

5. What constructions will probably follow **ut**, if it is meant
   (a) as conjunction?
   (b) as adverb?
   (a) A substantive purpose clause.
   (b) A noun (appositive), adjective, or adjectival phrase, belonging to the personal subject or object of **persuadet**,
   and so nom. or dat.

6. May be either of what possible parts of speech, and, in either
   case, in what construction?
   Noun, nom., subject of substantive final clause introduced by
   the *conjunction* **ut**; or, adjective, dat., agreeing with personal object of **persuadet**, and introduced by the *adverb* **ut**.

7. Does it call for anything to complete its meaning, and, if so,
   what?
   An objective genitive.

8. What three uses has the word **et**?
   (1) Connecting two words, = *and*; (2) as the first of two ets
   = *both . . . and*; or (3) as bearing upon a single word, =
   also, even.　　　　　\

9. What uses may et have, in each case, in the present passage?
   It may connect **cupido**, or **honorum**, to something yet to
   come; or it may be the first of two balanced ets; or it
   may emphasize a word or phrase to follow.

10. What is now the probable meaning of **et**, what its office, and
    what light does it throw upon **cupido**? Mark the quan-
    tity of the i in the last.
    And; connecting the **cui**-sentence to **cupĭdo**, which is an
    adjective.

11. If this surmise is right, then what part of speech will the **cui**-
    sentence be equivalent to, and by what mode will this
    meaning be expressed?
    An adjective; expressed by the *characterizing* mode, the sub-
    junctive.

12. Is name of town in nom. pl.? What three possibilities of con-
    struction?
    Subject, predicate, or in apposition with the one or the
    other.

13. Part of speech and possible cases?
Adjective, nom. sing. fem., abl. sing. fem., nom. or acc. neut. pl.
14. Meaning of its position before its noun?
That it is emphatic.
15. Possible parts of speech, and corresponding meanings?
Adjective, meaning *so great*, or adverb, meaning *to such a degree*, or *to such a degree and no further*, i.e. *only*.
16. In the last sense, what are its synonyms?
Solum and **modo**.
17. What part of speech was **tantum**, and what did it modify?
Adverb, modifying **materna**.
18. Probable construction of **patria** and of **Tarquinii**?
Tarquinii is probably subject of the **cui**-verb, and **patria** its predicate.
19. Write the verb.
Esset.
20. Where made?
Participle, dat. or abl. pl.
21. Possible cases?
Dat. or abl.
22. Probable construction?
Ablative absolute with **sublatis.**
23. The place they go to is Rome. Complete the sentence in two ways, using **urbs** in one, and **Roma** in the other.
Ad urbem; Romam.
24. Translate the passage.

SECOND EXERCISE (Livy I. 9, 1).

[Romulus has enclosed a great space with his fortifications, and gathered a crowd of refugees into his new city.]

Iam res[1] Romana[2] adeo[3] erat[4][5] valida, ut cuilibet[6][7] finitimarum[8] civitatum bello[9][10][11] par[12][13] ——; sed penuria[14][15] mulierum hominis aetatem[16] duratura[17][18] magnitudo[19][20] ——, quippe[21] quibus[22][23][24][25][26] nec[27] domi[28] spes[29] prolis nec cum finitimis conubia[30] ——[31].

1. Possible cases?
   Nom. sing., nom. or acc. pl.
2. Probable case and construction of **res**?
   Nom., subject of main verb.
3. Commonest meaning of **adeo**? and how must its meaning, if completed, be completed?
   To such a degree; by consecutive **ut**-sentence.
4. Meaning of the tense?
   State of affairs at the point which the story has reached.
5. What two parts of speech are capable of completing the sentence?
   Adjective and participle.
6. Part of speech? what other word is substantially equivalent?
   Indefinite pronoun; **cuivis**.
7. How are we to think of the meaning of case?
   As some aspect of the indirect object.
8. Suggests the beginning of what construction?
   Partitive genitive.
9. Possible cases and possible constructions?
   Dative of some aspect of the indirect object, or ablative in some instrumental aspect.
10. Can **cuilibet** go with **bello**, and why?
    No; for the partitive genitive shows that **cuilibet** refers to a **civitati**.
11. Then is **bello** more likely to turn out to be a dative, or an ablative?
    An ablative.
12. What suspense about Livy's meaning is now resolved?
    Cuilibet is the dative of the indirect object to which the quality of **par** is directed, and **bello** is the ablative of respect for **par**.
13. Write the predicate from **sum**.
    Esset.
14. Possible cases?
    Nom. or abl.
15. If the idea is completed, by what case?
    Objective genitive.
16. Possible meanings of the case?
    Duration of time, appositive, object of a verb, or subject or predicate of an infinitive.

17. Probable meaning of case of **aetatem**?
Duration of time.
18. What two possibilities for the government of **duratura**?
That it belongs (1) to **penuria**, or (2) to something not yet arrived.
19. What do we now feel about the case of **penuria**, and the meaning of that case?
That it is an ablative, expressing the cause of **duratura**.
20. Write predicate from **sum**, choosing the tense with care.
Erat.
21. Conceive of **quippe** as an adverb, meaning *indeed, in fact.*
22. What is the probable nature of the **quibus**-sentence, and what its construction?
Adjectival, *i.e.*, a characterizing sentence in subjunctive.
23. What must be the underlying relation between the condition of affairs which we shall find expressed in the **quibus**-sentence, and the condition of affairs expressed in the main sentence?
Causal.
24. What is the antecedent of **quibus**?
The people to whom the **magnitudo** belonged, the inhabitants of the town.
25. Possible cases?
Dat. or abl.
26. **Quibus** indicates persons. How does that narrow the possibilities of an ablative construction?
It can be only abl. absolute, or ablative dependent on a comparative or some word like **fretus** or **contentus**, or ablative of source with some word like **genitus, ortus, natus.**
27. What is sure about **nec**?
That it balances a later **nec** or **et.**
28. Construction?
Locative.
29. What must follow?
Objective genitive or future infinitive.
30. Complete the sentence by writing the proper form from the verb **sum.**
Essent.
31. Translate.

THIRD EXERCISE (Livy I. 24, 2).

[The Alban and Roman kings have proposed that the war between the two peoples shall be settled by a battle between the Horatii and Curiatii.]

Nihil recusatur. Tempus et locus convenit. Priusquam[12] dimicareut, foedus ictum[3] inter Romanos et Albanos est his[4][5] legibus[6], ut cuius[7][8] populi cives[9] eo certamine vicissent[10] is alteri[11][12] populo cum bona pace[13] ____[14].

1. What ideas may one have in mind when he writes **antequam** or **priusquam**, and by what mode will these ideas be respectively expressed?

   He may mean to give the idea of an act anticipated — *i.e.*, looked forward to from the time of the act of the main clause — by some person mentioned in that sentence; and he will express this by the *idea-mode*, the subjunctive. Or he may mean to state the actual occurrence of an event, as a boundary point *beyond which* the main event took place; and he will express this by the *fact-mode*, the indicative.

2. In the light of the situation, which of the two ideas is it more probable that Livy is going to express?

   The former.

3. Is anything sure yet about the case of **foedus**, or the part of speech of **ictum**?

   No.

4. What should be kept in mind as possibilities for all demonstrative pronominal words, like **is, hic, ille, ita,** etc.?

   That they look backward to something already mentioned, or forward to something which is yet to be mentioned.

5. Which is the case here?

   The latter.

6. What construction do you think is coming?

   A substantive final clause, telling what the **his legibus** were.

7. In general, what have we found to be the two possibilities when one meets the combination of **ut** and the relative?

Either (1) that **ut** is the conjunction, and the **qui**-clause looks forward to an antecedent to be given later in the **ut**-clause; or (2) that **ut** is the adverb, the **qui** looking backward, and the relative statement forming a characterizing clause which stands in a causal relation to the main clause.

8. Bearing in mind **his legibus**, which of the two possible meanings of the combination **ut cuius** do you suppose to have been in Livy's mind in this particular case?

The former.

9. Probable meaning of case of **populi**?

Possessive, depending on **cives**.

10. Meaning of tense?

Future perfect from a past point of view.

11. Probable nature of combination?

Subject and indirect object.

12. Differs how in meaning from *alius*?

Refers to the one other out of two, while *alius* means *another* out of any number.

13. Surmise, if possible, what the final verb is; and at any rate tell where it must be made.

Imperfect subjunctive; **imperaret** (*imperaret* is likely to be written rather than Livy's frequentative *imperitaret;* but the word is admissible).

14. Translate.

FOURTH EXERCISE (Livy XXII. 38, 1).

[The year following the defeat at the Trasumene lake. Dissatisfaction with the policy of Fabius. The people have carried the election of one consul, Varro, the nobility of the other, Aemilius Paullus. The two are about to march out for the summer campaign.]

Contiones[1] priusquam[2] ab urbe signa moverentur[3] consulis[4] Varronis multae ac feroces fuere, denuntiantis[5][6] bellum[7][8][9] arcessitum[10] in[11] Italiam ab nobilibus mansurumque[12] in[13] visceribus reipublicae, si[14] plurcs Fabios imperatores haberet, se[15] quo die[16] hostem vidisset[17] perfecturum.[18][19]

1. Possible meanings?
   Meeting, and *speech* made before a meeting.
2. What meanings may follow, and by what constructions indicated?
   Action anticipated at the time of the main act, expressed by the subjunctive; or actual event, back of which the main act lies, expressed by the indicative.
3. What was the special shade of meaning in **priusquam . . moverentur**?
   That the **contiones** were held, or made, in anticipation of the expected marching.
4. What is it now clear that **contiones** means?
   Means *speech, harangue.*
5. Belongs with what?
   Consulis.
6. **Denuntiare** means to make an announcement. How will the object be expressed if it is
   (*a*) a noun or pronoun?
   (*b*) a verb, conveying a statement of fact?
   (*c*) a verb, conveying action desired?
   (*a*) Accusative.
   (*b*) Infinitive.
   (*c*) Substantive final clause.
7. What construction occurs to you at once for **bellum**?
   Object of **denuntiantis.**
8. Is there any certainty that this is what Livy meant?
   No.
9. What else may Livy have in mind?
   A subject or an object for an infinitive depending upon **denuntiantis.**
10. What possibilities for **arcessitum**?
    Participle agreeing with **bellum**, or part of an infinitive perfect (with *esse* to come) or future (with *iri* to come) having **bellum** for its subject.
11. What case do you expect to find following, and why?
    Accusative, because **arcessitum** includes the idea of motion.
12. What is the only thing that you know surely about **mansurum**?

That its construction is the same as that of **arcessitum**.

13. What case do you expect to find following, and why?
Ablative, because **mansurum** includes the idea of rest.

14. What indication have you of the probable nature of the condition, and how will it be expressed?
It looks as if it were the condition for **mansurum**. In that
case it will be a future or future perfect from the past
standpoint, expressed by the so-called imperfect or plu-
perfect subjunctive.

15. Probable construction of **bellum** and **arcessitum**, and grounds
of your opinion?
Se is acc. or abl. It cannot be abl. absolute, since it refers to
the subject of the sentence; and it is probably not the
ablative of source, for we are not likely to find a word
meaning *born of* here. It is therefore probably accusative.
In that case, **bellum** is either the subject or object of an
active infinitive which we are to have, and of which **se** is
object or subject. **Arcessitum**, which is passive, is therefore not an infinitive, but a participle; and, beside that,
mansurum, which is in the same construction with
arcessitum, is not transitive.

16. Where is the antecedent of **quo die**, and what do you know
about it?
Yet to come, and in some way connected with the coming infinitive which we have found to depend upon **denuntiantis**.

17. Meaning of tense and mode?
Future perfect from past point of view, in indirect discourse.

18. What suspended constructions are now resolved?
Perfecturum is infinitive, **se** its subject, **bellum** its object,
with attached participles **arcessitum** and **mansurum**,
the latter having a future condition dependent upon it.

19. Translate.

FIFTH EXERCISE (Livy XXI. 53, 1).

[The passage here used was employed in the address. It is given again in its
place among the present set of papers, partly to show that the minute questioning
with which a teacher of an untrained Freshman class must begin may give place
early to a more rapid movement, after the habit of watchfulness and a willingness to
hold the mind in suspense have been established.]

Hannibal cum quid[1] optimum foret hoste cerneret, vix[2] ullam spem[3] habebat temere[4][5] atque improvide[6] —— consules[7][8] —— ; cum alterius ingenium, fama[9] prius deinde re[10] cognitum, percitum ac ferox sciret[11] ——, ferociusque factum prospero cum praedatoribus[12] suis certamine crederet, adesse gerendae rei fortunam haud diffidebat.[13]

1. What must be the construction of the verb of the **quid**-sentence, and why?

   Subjunctive of indirect question of fact, or of indirect deliberative question.

2. In such a connection, what would be the pronoun meaning *any*, and what the adjective?

   Quisquam, ullus.

3. What would be the completing construction (*a*) if nominal?[1]

                                  (*b*) if verbal?

   (*a*) Genitive.

   (*b*) Genitive of gerund or of gerundive, or future infinitive.

4. Does **temere**, judging by the order, probably modify **habebat**, or something yet to come.

   The latter.

5. Then what do you surmise about the completing construction for **spem**?

   That it is a verbal construction.

6. Write the neuter pronoun meaning *anything*, in nom. or acc. form.

   Quicquam.

7. General construction hereby indicated, and construction of **consules** and of the word you have just written?

   The verbal for **spem** is an infinitive, with **quicquam** for subject and **consules** for object, or *vice versa*.

---

[1] It would be a practical convenience if there were an adjective bearing the same relation to the words *noun* and *pronoun* that *verbal* bears to *verb*. For my own use I have employed the adjective *nominal* in this sense.

8. Write the infinitive, meaning *to do*.
Acturos.

9. Case?
Nom. or abl.

10. Case of **fama**, and proof.
Abl., because the phrase **prius deinde** makes it parallel with **re**.

11. Write verb required to complete the clause.
Esse.

12. What is indicated by a combination like **prospero cum praedatoribus**?
That **cum** connects with **praedatoribus** a noun, yet to come, to which **prospero** belongs.

13. Translate.

SIXTH EXERCISE (Livy XXII. 40, 1).

Adversus[1] ea[2] oratio[3] consulis haud sane laeta fuit, magis fatentis[4] ea[5] quae diceret vera quam facilia[6] ——[7] ——: dictatori magistrum[8][9] equitum intolerabilem fuisse; quid[10][11] consuli adversus collegam seditissum ac temerarium verium atque auctoritatis[12] —— ?[13]

1. What part of speech is **adversus**?
Participle or preposition.

2. What is possible for **ea**?
Object of preposition **adversus**, or agreeing with an abl. sing. or acc. pl.

3. What do you know now about **adversus** and **ea**, and how?
Oratio is nom. fem., so that **adversus** is not participle, but preposition, **ea** being its object.

4. Construction to follow (*a*) if nominal?
(*b*) if verbal?
(*a*) Accusative.
(*b*) Infinitive statement in indirect discourse.

5. Possible constructions?
Object of **fatentis**, or subject or predicate of an infinitive depending on it.

6. Write Latin for *to do*, completing the idea of **facilia**.
   Factu.
7. Write in Latin whatever is still necessary to complete the sentence.
   Esse.
8. Meaning of the position of **dictatori** and **magistrum**?
   Sharp contrast.
9. Probable general construction of sentence?
   Indirect statement, in the infinitive, **magistrum** being its subject, and **dictatori** being the indirect object of the infinitive, or of a predicate adjective.
10. In the present construction, what modes possible after **quid**, and with what meanings respectively?
    Subjunctive of indirect question, either deliberative or seriously asking for information, or infinitive, in rhetorical question practically amounting to an assertion.[1]
11. If a partitive genitive is to follow, in what part of the clause have we learned that we are likely to find it?
    As far removed from the word on which it depends as the other points of style will allow.
12. Decide, in the light of the whole passage, what kind of a sentence this necessarily is, and write the Latin for *would there be*.
    Fore, or futurum esse.
13. Translate.

---

[1] It is of course unadvisable, for class-work of this sort, to cover at the beginning all the possibilities of the indirect interrogative sentence. I have given such of them as are easily grasped and are most important.

APPLICATION OF THE METHOD IN PREPARATORY WORK.

It will be convenient to refer, in these suggestions, to some one of the books commonly employed by beginners in Latin; *e.g.*, Dr. Leighton's "First Steps in Latin." The application can of course be made with ease to any other book of the same scope.

First and most important is it that the beginner should accustom himself from the very outset to the sound of the Roman language. In Lesson XIII., *e.g.*, the learner, having prepared himself upon the sentences **regina laudat, scribae portant, puellae laudant, laudas, laudamus, reginae donant**, etc., should not open his book to translate them. *His book should be closed*, and he should give the meaning of **regina laudat**, etc., as his teacher delivers the sentence to him. To translate **regina laudat** *at hearing*, after having studied it, *is not beyond the mental power of the modern boy.* Neither is it beyond his power, with possibly a trifle of patience on the part of his teacher, to translate at hearing a *new* sentence of the same scope, *e.g.*, **laudo; scriba laudat; scriba donat; scribae donant.** But if this is true, a very important truth at once follows. There is, it will be admitted, no greater jump in any first Latin book than that from nothing at all to the first lesson in Latin sentences of one and two words. If, in taking that step, the boy can successfully prepare himself to translate the set lesson at hearing, and to translate in the same way new sentences of the same vocabulary and the same scope, then *he can prepare* *himself, as he progresses by carefully graded steps,* in any of the books in common use, *to translate any previously studied Latin at hearing, and to translate at hearing any new sentences of the same scope, framed for him by the invention of his teacher.* Before the book is opened by any one but the teacher, the exercises of the class-room should be (1) the translation at hearing of the review, (2) the translation at hearing of the advance, and (3) the translation at hearing of new sentences of the same scope. And no one will venture to say that a boy who had been carried in this way through an introductory book would not begin Cæsar as a better Latinist than a boy who had not been so started.

In Lesson XIII., as we have seen, the boy has learned that the subject of a verb is expressed by the nominative. In the next lesson he is told that the direct object of a transitive verb is expressed by the accusative. For the present, that is the sum total of his knowledge about accusatives. Of course the teacher will narrow his own knowledge to his pupil's horizon. Accordingly, he will start upon a sentence beginning with an accusative, *e.g.* **scribas**, and ask the learner what, without hearing the rest of the sentence, he learns from the *case*, with regard to the relation of the *clerks* to the rest of the sentence; in a word, what the *meaning* of the case is. The boy will answer "*object of the verb*," and the teacher will accept the answer. Then he will give the beginning of another sentence, containing a nominative and an accusative, say **regina scribam**, and ask the learner what the two cases mean to him. The learner will answer *subject* and *object*. The teacher will then give a number of combinations of subject and

object, *e.g.* **scriba puellam, nauta agricolam,** employing the full vocabulary provided in the lesson. Then,
retracing his steps, he will give complete sentences of
which the combinations just used may be supposed to
be the beginning, repeating each of these combinations
in connection with as many as possible of the various
verbs provided ; *e.g.,* **regina scribam laudat, regina
scribam vocat, regina scribam exspectat.** Then another combination, *e.g.* **scriba puellam,** should similarly
be repeated with various verbs. In all this, the Latin
should be given deliberately,[1] so that the pupil may be
able to form his mental pictures easily, as he hears one
word after another. He should be urged, too, to form
these pictures without thinking of the English word.
The word **regina** should bring a **regina** before his
mental vision, instead of bringing, first the *word* **queen,**
and then a mental vision of a queen.[2]

[1] The teacher who uses the Roman method should be fastidious in
his pronunciation, for his own example will tell far more than precept.
Now that every method-book has every syllable marked, there is no
possible justification for incorrectness. Yet many teachers, coming to
rēgīna and **amīcĭtiam** in Lesson XIV. will pronounce them **rĕgīna,
ămīcĭtiam** ; not a few will read **vŏcant** as **vōcant** ; and, I sadly fear,
nearly all, while teaching their students that final *a* is long in the
ablative and short in the nominative, etc., will pronounce **fāmă** and
fāmā precisely alike, namely as ablative, — though the sound of short
final *a* is very well represented to us in English in such familiar words
as Californiă, Nevadă, Cubă.

[2] I find teachers to be sceptical about the possibility of doing this.
But it is not even difficult, if the young student begins rightly and is
rightly helped throughout. The apparent difficulty goes back to the
false habits of mind produced by making *translation* the constant
method of getting at the meaning of the author, and, so to speak, the
ultimate end of study ; whereas the true end of study, precisely as in
the case of modern languages, is to get the power to *read the original.*

In these exercises there should be no translation into English (it will be remembered that the Latin of the review and the Latin of the advance have already been translated at hearing). Next should come an exercise like the following: "How, in Latin, can you present to my mind a queen as acting upon somebody?" *By saying* **rēgīnă**. "How a girl as being acted upon?" *By saying* **puellam**. "How a clerk?" *By saying* **scrībam**. "How a letter?" *By sáying* **epistulam**. "Now put before me a queen as acting, and a girl as being acted upon." **Rēgīna puellam**. "A farmer as acting, and a sailor as being acted upon." **Agricolă nautam**. After a number of these combinations have been given, "Now tell me in Latin that the queen is waiting for the clerk," then "that the queen is waiting for the letter," etc., etc. Variations of the tense of the verb should also be employed. I must confine myself, however, to showing the method of dealing with the cases.

In the next lesson, XVI., the pupil will learn one of the simple uses of the genitive. He should then be asked what the cases tell him in **liber pueri** (being made, of course, to see that, though **pueri** might be nom. pl. so far as form goes, it cannot be so here, since **liber** must be subject), in **magister reginae filiam**, etc. ;

It is to be feared, even, that, in the pressure produced by the long hours of their working day, many teachers in the preparatory schools do not themselves read the authors they teach, but only make preparation to correct the students' translations at the recitations. If they would devote five minutes a day to reading their Cæsar, Virgil, and Cicero aloud, as before an imaginary audience, and five minutes more to doing the same thing before a real audience in their class-room, they would find their faith to grow apace.

and should then be carried through various exercises similar to those suggested in connection with the previous lesson. He will also learn in Lesson XVI. about apposition, of which more anon. In Lesson XVII. he will learn about the way of expressing the *indirect* object of a verb, and should now be asked what the cases mean in combinations like **agricolae nautis viam, nauta agricolis viam, scriba puero librum, scriba pueris reginae libros, agricola puero scribae viam,** etc.; and should then have whole sentences given him, and English combinations and sentences to be put into Latin, as already described.

So constructions are taught one after another, the simplest meaning of each case being alone given when the case is first dealt with. Later, other uses of these same cases are taught, and the certainty which the pupil at first felt in regard to the speaker's meaning when he heard a given case (say the accusative) now passes away. As early as Lesson XVI. he learned, as we saw, that "a noun used to describe another noun or pronoun, and meaning the same thing, is put in the same case." At this point, consequently, he recognizes that there is a double possibility for a given accusative. Supposing us to take up a sentence beginning (say) with **legatum,** the accusative word may turn out to be either of two things, namely, the *object* of the verb, or in *apposition* to the object of the verb. These two possibilities, and these alone, should, for a number of weeks, flash through the beginner's mind at sight or hearing of an accusative. Later, however (Lessons LI. and LII.), he will find that certain verbs are of such a nature as to take *two objects*, and will have specimens given him. At this point an accusative has for him *three* possibilities : it may be, to the speaker's thought, *object*, it may be *second object*, or it may be an *appositive;* while if the meaning of the words is such as to exclude all possibility of the last of these, as, *e.g.*, in a sentence beginning with **me fraudem**, the meaning of the combination is seen at once to be that **me** is the first object, and **fraudem** the second object, of some one of the verbs that need two objects to complete their thought, *e.g.* **celo**. Not long afterward, he will learn (Lesson LXI.) about the accusative of *duration of time* and *extent of space*, and he now must recognize still another possibility for any accusatives like **annos** or **pedes**, but *not* for a word like **Caesarem** or **me**. Still later, he will add to his repertory an understanding of the *cognate accusative*, of the *accusative as subject of an infinitive*, etc. The teacher will keep clearly before the learner's mind that, while any accusative may be a direct object, or the subject or predicate of an infinitive, only words of a particular meaning can be used in the expression of duration of time, etc., and only words of another and an equally particular meaning can play the part of a cognate accusative, etc. The teacher would do well to make for himself, as the book progressed, a collection of short sentences illustrating all the possible kinds of accusatives (as yet known to the pupil) in which a given word, like **Caesarem, annos, vitam**, may occur (and, of course, similar collections for the other cases) ; and to run through one of these collections frequently, perhaps daily, with the class, using no English. Throughout this progress, it will be noted, *nothing has been allowed* *to lapse.* The way described of looking at all the possible meanings of (say) an accusative, seen or heard, constitutes a continual review of the sharpest nature, and, furthermore, of that very persuasive and pressing kind which looks toward immediate and constant practical use.

Following these methods, the pupil will surely, if the exercises of translating at hearing and understanding at hearing without translating are kept up, have obtained, by the time he reaches the end of the book, the power to catch the force of the accusative constructions, in short and simple sentences, with correctness and *without conscious operations of reasoning.* For his very familiarity with all the possibilities of accusative constructions for words of one and another meaning will have brought him into a condition in which, on the one side, he will WAIT, OPEN-MINDED, for the word or words that shall determine which meaning the speaker had in his own thought (if, as mostly, those words are yet to come); and, on the other, will, by a tact now grown unconscious, INSTINCTIVELY APPREHEND, when the determining word or words arrive, what that meaning was; in short, he will have made a good beginning of understanding the Roman language as it was understood by Roman hearers and Roman readers.

The sketch here given for the treatment of the accusative constructions suggests the way in which any set of constructions should be managed. I append a few specimens of the results for this and that class of words in a number of cases. I grant that the enumeration for the ablative, and even for the genitive, is of provoking sweep; but this is only equivalent to saying that the number of meanings of the ablative and genitive cases which a young student must learn, under whatsoever method, is great.

The genitive of any pronoun may be found to mean *the possessor* of some *thing* or of some *activity* (the activity being expressed in a verbal noun), or *the object of some activity* (expressed in a noun, an adjective, or some one of a certain list of verbs), or *the whole* of which some other word expresses a part, — may be, then, either *subjective*, or *objective*, or *partitive;* or it may simply belong to some noun, just as an adjective does. The genitive of any noun (say **civitatis**) may prove to be either *subjective*, or *objective*, or *partitive*, or *in apposition* with some other genitive. The genitive of a noun like **periculi** may prove to be either *appositive*, or *subjective*, or *objective*, or *partitive*, or (if modified by a noun or participle) *qualitative*. The genitive of a noun indicating an *act or mental state of a bad nature* may be either *appositive*, or *subjective*, or *objective*, including *a crime charged or a penalty adjudged*, or may be *partitive*. A genitive **magni** may agree with a noun, or may mean the *value* of something.

The dative of any word may mean *the person or thing indirectly concerned* in an act or state expressed by a noun or an adjective or a group of words. The dative of the name of a person (say **Caesari**) may have this general meaning, or, in one or another special phase of it, may mean the *person concerned in an obligation* indicated by a gerundive (*the agent*), or *the possessor* of something. The dative of a word like **dolori, laudi,** etc., may mean, in a general way, the thing indirectly concerned, or, with a special phase of that idea, may mean the *end served*.

The accusative we have discussed already. The voc-
ative takes care of itself, when the form is unmis-
takable.

The ablative is a case to be dreaded. In general, it
should, like other cases, be cut up as little as possible.
Something can be done by proceeding from the three
ideas of the *starting-point*, the *means*, and the *place*
(*true ablative*, *instrumental*, and *locative*), as in Dr.
Leighton's table on p. 290, and the table on p. 254 of
the Allen & Greenough Grammar; but the best inten-
tions on the part of grammarians and teachers have
not yet made the matter easy for the learner. The suggestions to be given here must go beyond these three
divisions.

Nearly all ablatives can be *absolute*, or can depend
upon a *comparative*, or on a word like *dignus* or *contentus*. Beside this, a proper name (say **Caesare**) may
be in the ablative of *source*, after some word like *genitus*, though such a form of expression is naturally rare
in the prose read before going to college. Of course
such a word cannot be in the ablative of *means* (in the
narrower sense), or of *specification*, or of *time*, or of
degree of difference. A word like **die**, however, beside
the general possibilities, may indicate *time*, or the *degree of difference*, a word like **auro** *means* or *price*, a
word like **capite** *description*, etc. I shall not attempt
here a complete list of suggestions. In general, in spite
of the complexity of the uses of the ablative, the learner
is less likely to go badly astray in dealing with this case
in actual practice than in dealing with the genitive or
the accusative.

One point not yet touched upon is of the gravest

consequence. When a form occurs which may be in either of two cases, or even possibly in any one of three or four cases, the pupil should not allow himself to suppose that he knows the case, even if a probability presents itself at once. *E.g.*, a student reading in B. G. 1, 3, and passing by *ea* (*his rebus adducti et auctoritate Orgetorigis permoti constituerunt ea, quae*, etc.), may easily suppose *ea* to be the object of *constituerunt*, instead of waiting until conviction of some kind is forced upon him by the remainder of the sentence; which conviction will prove to be that *ea* was the object, not of *constituerunt*, but of an infinitive which is not reached until the *quae*-clause is finished. The direction to the student should be: *Have your eyes open, but keep in doubt as long as possible;* in a word, THINK and WAIT.

Verbal constructions should be dealt with in a similar way. The possibilities after conjunctions should, in particular, be entirely familiar. Given a *quamquam* or a *quamvis*, the student should be able to tell instantly what is coming. Given an *antequam*, he should know precisely what the two ideas are, either one of which may possibly be in the speaker's mind, and by what mode each was expressed by the Romans. Given an *ut*, he should know the full range of ideas possible for the speaker to have when he so begins a clause, and by what construction each of these ideas is expressed. And in particular it will be found useful to set before the class the whole range of verbal constructions that are capable of serving as the object or the subject of a verb (substantive clauses), and to ask them which and how many of these a given verb or phrase may take. These substantive clauses are as follows: —

The indirect statement of fact (infinitive).
The indirect question of fact.
The indirect deliberative question..
The final clause.
The consecutive clause.

Now give the class a verb, **dicit**, and ask what possible completing verbal ideas there may be, and what phase of meaning one and another of these would indicate for the word **dicit** itself. The answer should be: the infinitive, if **dicit** means that a statement is made; the subjunctive introduced by an interrogative (including of course **ut**), if **dicit** means the giving of an answer to a question of fact or a deliberate question; the subjunctive with **ut** or **ne**, if **dicit** means the giving of a direction. The substantive consecutive clause, it is, of course, impossible for **dicit** to take. On the other hand, the meaning of a word like **efficit** is such that it can take the substantive consecutive clause and can take no other; so that, unless we find a clear accusative object, we are sure, upon meeting an **efficit**, that a verbal object introduced by **ut** or **ut non** is sooner or later to come. A verb like **peto** can take only a substantive final clause, a verb like **quaero** only an interrogative substantive clause (either a question of fact, or a deliberative question), etc. To look at these matters in this particular way is of great usefulness. If, for example, the class is translating at hearing, in Cat. Mai. 63, the anecdote beginning **quin etiam memoriae proditum est**, everybody should at this point instantly recognize that an infinitive of statement is sooner or later inevitable, and, knowing the Latin habit of arrangement, *should at once associate with that impending*

infinitive statement all the intervening matter, **cum Athe-
nis ludis quidam in theatrum**, etc.   The same thing
is seen, with a much briefer suspense, in Cæsar's **id si
fieret, intellegebat magno cum periculo**, etc., B. G.
1, 10, 2.

Most of the things thus far mentioned will be familiar
to the student before he leaves his introductory book
and begins Cæsar.   At this point, he takes up sentences
more complex, and yet in the main containing no new
principles.   His teacher can now do him a great service
by reading aloud both familiar and new sentences, in
such a way as to throw the parts into masses; and by
teaching the student to do the same in what he has
already read.   *E.g.*, in B. G. 1, 8, the words **ea legione
quam secum habebat** form one idea, and should be
given without separation; the words **militibusque qui
ex provincia convenerant** form another, connected,
after a slight pause, with the former group; the sentence **qui fines Sequanorum ab Helvetiis dividit**
should be delivered as a single mass, and in such a
manner as to ·show that it is a piece of parenthetical
explanation.   In this way, the teacher can make his
hearers feel that this longish sentence of five lines, with
its verb held up to the last place, is really entirely
simple.   He should also call attention to the very
common pointings-forward to an explanatory sentence,
which are effected by pronouns and pronominal adverbs,
as, *e.g.*, in **id** in 1, 31, 2 (**non minus se id contendere**)
which, as the meaning of **contendere** tells us, must be
explained to us later in a substantive purpose clause;
as in **hoc** in 1, 32, 4 (**respondit hoc esse miseriorem et
graviorem fortunam**), which must be explained later

either by a **quo** in a sentence containing another comparative, or by a **quod**-sentence containing a statement of fact; as in **haec** in 1, 40, 11 (**haec sibi esse curae**), which must be explained by a substantive final clause, or by an infinitive; as in an **ita**, looking forward to an **ut**- or **si**-clause, or an infinitive; etc., etc.

The teacher will all the while know very well what things his class is familiar with, and what it is not familiar with, and will accordingly drop questionings upon the former and continue them upon the latter. But up to the very end, there should be stated exercises in translation at hearing, say once a week, with careful questions upon points critical for the apprehension of the meaning; the passages themselves to be committed to memory later. This is the most effective engine of the method, — the surest way of developing and keeping up the habits of watchfulness and of willingness to wait.

And now a brief summary of suggestions, in which I will address myself directly to the teacher.

At the outset, make the student feel that the Latin language was once an every-day tongue of men, women, and children; a tongue in which people not only wrote books, but dined, and played tennis; a language spoken, and understood as spoken. Direct him, therefore, to aim to associate meaning with the *sound* of the word, not merely with groups of letters on a page. Tell him, as he commits his vocabulary to memory, to lift his eye from the printed word, and repeat again and again, in imagination, the spoken word, so that when he hears it from his teacher, he will feel its force immediately.

Throughout the introductory lesson-book, conduct the translation of the review and of the advance at hearing, and, in the same way, have the student, his book being closed, put the printed English sentences into Latin as you deliver them to him. If you do this from the first, he will be able, by the time the lesson-book is finished, to express a sentence of considerable length in Latin, grasping it as a whole, instead of turning one word into Latin, and then another, and so on, in piecemeal fashion.

If you can get time for preparation, aim at repetition, making for your own use, in connection with each lesson in the book, a group of sentences which, employing the vocabulary already acquired, shall proceed from change to change with but a slight difference each time. A simple example of what I mean may be recalled from pp. 56 and 58.[1] In this matter, — the insisting upon the value of repetition, — the Sauveur method is quite right.

As the student learns one new use after another, say of the accusative, help him to get a clear and practically serviceable idea of the possibilities of range of one and another kind of word, as **Caesarem, mille passuum, annum, multum.**

In a similar way, help him to classify ideas that are expressed by verbal constructions, especially in subordinate clauses. Let him, for example, know with perfect

---

[1] I question whether it would not be better to use a smaller vocabulary in the first few lessons than some of the books employ, aiming rather, by the varied repetition of a comparatively few words in the simple constructions of subject, direct object, indirect object, and predicate, at giving the student a real facility in the grasping of meanings and the conveying of meanings through inflections. It is hard for the young mind to get this facility when dealing with things so new if it is encumbered at the same time with having to handle a large vocabulary.

familiarity what two kinds of adversative ideas exist in the nature of things, and by what mode these are respectively expressed in Latin (of the period which he is dealing with), and with what introductory particles. Let him know familiarly what two ideas one may have in mind in using an *antequam*-construction, a *dum*-construction, and so on, and how these ideas are expressed.

By the time he has finished the introductory book, he will in this way have made the intelligent acquaintance of very nearly all the constructions of the language, and should have them all in working order, like familiar tools.

When you come to Cæsar, do not let your class make the first plunge alone, but for a number of days carry them through the advance yourself, avoiding translation on your own part as far as possible, reading the Latin to them in your very best and most helpful manner, and pointing out order and construction. Throughout the Cæsar and Cicero (I should say precisely the same thing of the Anabasis) have the review of each day prepared to be translated at hearing. Encourage your students to learn to deliver the Latin well by appointing a promising reader, from time to time, to prepare himself in advance to read the review to the class in your stead. Let him stand at your side with his eye upon his fellow-students; and as he finishes a sentence, or such part of a sentence as shall be best to give in a lump, do you yourself name the student who shall translate.

Be sure that you constantly treat constructions as *means of expressing certain ideas*, not as mere exemplifications of rules. And, to enforce this view, as well as for many other reasons, watch constantly the development of ideas in dealing with sentences which your students have not seen before, and, in your questioning for written answers, or for *viva voce* answers, call attention to point after point in the gradual unfolding of the meaning, demanding all the time what I have elsewhere called *anticipatory parsing*. And have a good deal of memorizing and reciting of these selected passages.

Aim to go a little beyond the lesson every day, having your class read on, not at sight, but at hearing, this additional ground being understood to form a part of the review at the next meeting.

The disadvantage of reading on at sight is twofold. The student is too apt to look ahead while some one else is up, preparing himself to make a good showing if he is called upon. And even if he does not do this, he is too ready to run his eye to and fro in the sentence, not really accepting the Latin order, but doing a more or less clever piece of rapid patchwork. It often happens to me, in dealing with students who have been well practised in sight-reading before coming to the University, to read aloud a sentence containing only familiar words, every one of which they catch as it is delivered, yet fail to get any meaning from the sentence as a whole; and I commonly find that, if I will at once put the sentence in the very same words, but in the English order, they will comprehend it instantly and without difficulty. That experience proves that one may do a deal of sight-reading, yet never come to know the Latin order in any practical way.[1]

[1] Here lies the answer to the question, What is the good of going through the extra difficulty of understanding Latin without seeing it, when all that we aim at is to be able to read the printed page? With-

Finally, no day should pass without composition. The writing of Latin is one of the most dreary of intellectual occupations, or one of the most delightful. Pretty uniformly it is the former for a boy who has not written a Latin sentence from the time he finished his elementary book and began his Cæsar till, only a few months before going to college, he took up his special book in composition for the bare purpose of preparing for the examination in that subject. The object of writing Latin in the preparatory schools is not to get one's self ready to pass an examination, but to get one's self ready to read Latin; and if that aim be intelligently pursued, the examination in writing Latin will take care of itself. The pursuit, however, should be incessant. Every day a number of sentences based

out saying anything about the greater sense of reality, and the greater interest which this way of dealing with the language brings with it, one might make the matter clear by supposing the case to be reversed. If English were a dead language, and Roman boys were learning to read it under Roman teachers who had mastered it, it would obviously be a very slow proceeding to pick it all to pieces and rearrange it into the Roman order as a means of understanding it. The most courteous ghost among us would laugh in the teacher's face if he were to visit a Roman schoolroom and find that sort of thing going on; just as undoubtedly the most courteous of Roman ghosts must laugh — unless, perhaps, his sense of grief over the waste of opportunity gets the better of his sense of humor — if ever he visits a modern schoolroom when a class is reading an oration of his great countryman. Just as he would surely say to us that this was precisely the way never to learn to read Latin, so our English-speaking ghost would beg the teacher to give all that business up, and to use some means to make it absolutely inevitable that the student should accept our English order of expression, to the end that he might really learn to read the language; and this means would necessarily be the trying to understand at hearing, first sentences of graded difficulty, then continuous passages of the literature.

upon the author in use at the time should be written by various members of the class, sent to the board for the purpose. Time can easily be obtained by having the writing going on while the class is reciting upon the review; after which, corrections should be called for from the class in general.

Throughout the work of the preparatory school, the teacher should insist upon it that what the pupil is primarily aiming at is to learn to read in a great literature, with as slight a barrier as possible between him and his author; and he should himself regard cases, modes, and tenses, and make his students regard them, as *keys to the literature*, as *direct conveyors of thought from mind to mind*. How the last may most effectively and rapidly be done, I have tried to show. This is all that strictly falls within the scope of the present pamphlet. But I cannot forbear to add that the teacher who is conducting a class through Cæsar, or Cicero, or Virgil, should never lose sight of the fact that his work is not wholly preparatory, — that *he is already dealing with a great literature*. The more he can make his students see that it is a great literature, through the virtue of his own enjoyment of it, and, in particular, through the power with which he can read it to them in the Latin, and the power with which he can train them to read it themselves, the easier will be his task, and the richer its palpable rewards; and the greater will be his contribution to the sum total of the classical education.

This brings us to the university, with its manifold aims, — the study of the literature and of the history of its development, the comparative study of the forms and the syntax, the study of ancient history from the sources, the study of ancient life, of ancient art, etc. All these various pursuits, however, rest ultimately mainly upon the power to read Latin with ease and speed.

Latin Text-Books.

Allen & Greenough's Latin Grammar.

A Latin Grammar for schools and colleges, founded on Comparative Grammar. By J. H. ALLEN, Lecturer at Harvard University, and J. B. GREENOUGH, Professor of Latin at Harvard University. 12mo. Half morocco. 348 pages. With new and greatly enlarged Index. Mailing price, $1.25; Introduction, $1.12; Allowance for old book, 45 cts.

The standing of this Grammar is now so well established that no extended comments or description need be given.

1. It has been used and recommended by teachers of Latin everywhere, — particularly in the large and in the distinctively classical schools, where an independent judgment might be expected.

2. Its firmest friends are those who have used it longest.

3. The clearness, simplicity, conciseness, convenience of size and arrangement, and economy of matter, essential in a class-room manual, have been secured without sacrifice of rigid scholarship, as is shown by the emphatic endorsements of eminent authorities.

4. To place before the public in authentic form the exact status of the question, the publishers print a series of testimonials from prominent professors and teachers, representing 132 colleges and 452 schools. The latter include about 72,000 students. These letters, which have a judicial value as the independent judgments of competent and disinterested men, pronounce the grammar

" Especially suited to beginners."   " Brief and concise."
" Broad, comprehensive, and complete."   " Simple and clear."
" Thorough, accurate, and scholarly."
" Systematic, scientific, and philosophical."
" Practical, and satisfactory to teachers and to students."
"**The best extant.**"   [*Send for the circular.*]

At the present time, inasmuch as the grammar has no longer against it the natural conservatism of the schools, and the no less natural prejudice of an entire corps of teachers trained in the methods of other books, its continued and increased success is not surprising.

Germania and Agricola of Tacitus.

Edited, for School and College Use, by W. F. ALLEN, Professor of Latin in the University of Wisconsin. 12mo. Cloth. 142 pages. Mailing Price, $1.10; Introduction, $1.00.

Clement L. Smith, *Prof. of Latin, Harvard College:* I used it with my class last year, and was greatly pleased with it. The notes are all excellent, and clearly expressed. (*Oct.* 9, 1881.)

Edwin Post, *Prof. of Latin, De Pauw University, Ind.:* It is the best text and. commentary for student use that I have ever used. (*Dec.* 2, 1881.)

Remnants of Early Latin.

Chiefly inscriptions. Selected and explained, for use in Colleges, by FREDERICK D. ALLEN, Professor of Classical Philology, Harvard College. Square 16mo. 106 pages. Mailing Price, 80 cents; Introduction, 75 cents.

THE object is to bring together, in small compass and convenient shape for reading, the most remarkable monuments of archaic Latin, with enough explanation to make them generally intelligible.

Cicero De Natura Deorum.

Libri Tres, with the Commentary of G. F. Schoemann, translated and edited by AUSTIN STICKNEY. 12mo. Cloth. 348 pages. Mailing Price, $1.55; Introduction, $1.40.

Tracy Peck, *Prof. of Latin, Yale College:* The value of Schoemann's edition has long been known, and I am glad that so careful a scholar as Professor Stickney has brought it to the easy reach of American students. The translator's additions, too, seem to be thoroughly helpful to a nicer understanding of the thought and Latinity of the original.

Selections from the Latin Poets.

With Notes for Colleges. Edited by E. P. CROWELL, Professor of Latin, Amherst College. 12mo. Cloth. 300 pages. Mailing Price, $1.55; Introduction, $1.40.

SELECTIONS are given from Catullus, Lucretius, Tibullus, Propertius, Ovid, and Lucan, with a sketch of the life and writings of each.

John K. Lord, *Prof. of Latin, Dartmouth College:* The selections indicate good taste and good judg- ment, and the notes are well adapted to their proposed end.

A Brief History of Roman Literature.

For Schools and Colleges. Translated and edited from the German edition of Bender by Professors E. P. Crowell and H. B. Richardson, of Amherst College. Square 16mo. 152 pages. Mailing Price, $1.10; Introduction, $1.00.

AN especial excellence of the work consists in its terse, suggestive, and admirable characterizations of the Roman writers and of their times. It contains just what the student ought to know, and suggests much for the teacher to enlarge upon.

W. A. Packard, *Prof. of Latin, Princeton College :* An excellent compendium, in translating and editing which the editors have done a good service.

A. G. Hopkins, *Prof. of Latin, Hamilton College :* It is the only satisfactory manual of the kind for the use of school and college with which I am acquainted.

Questions on Cæsar and Xenophon.

By E. C. Ferguson, Ph.D., Professor of Greek, McKendree College, Lebanon, Ill. 12mo. Cloth. iv + 283 pages. Mailing Price, $1.25; for introduction, $1.12.

GRAMMATICAL questions on the first book of Cæsar and the first of Xenophon with references to the grammars for the answers. (Allen & Greenough, and Harkness for the Latin; Goodwin, Hadley, and Hadley-Allen for the Greek.)

D. B. King, *Prof. of Latin, Lafayette, Coll..* I am much pleased with the general character of the questions, and have no doubt that the book will prove very suggestive to many teachers and to students as well.

Auxilia Vergiliana ; or, First Steps in Latin

Prosody.

By J. M. Whiton, Ph.D. 12mo. Paper cover. Mailing Price, 20 cents; Introduction, 15 cents.

INTENDED to facilitate the mastery of metre and rhythm at the very outset of the study of Latin Poetry.

A. H. Abbott, *Prin. of Little Blue School, Farmington, Me.:* I have never seen elsewhere Latin prosody made so plain. We shall at once adopt it.

Ginn & Company's Classical Atlas.

By A. KEITH JOHNSTON, LL.D., F.R.G.S., aided by the Rt. Honorable W. E. GLADSTONE, Prime Minister of England. Revised in 1885 with the co-operation of leading British and American scholars. Mailing Price, $2.30; for introduction, $2.00. See full description under the head of Geography.

Classical Wall Maps.

Engraved by W. & A. K. Johnston, Edinburgh. See the list and the prices, under the head of Geography.

King's Latin Pronunciation.

A brief outline of the Roman, Continental, and English methods, by D. B. KINO, formerly Professor of Latin in Lafayette College. 12mo. Cloth. 24 pages. Introduction Price, 25 cents.

The Latin Verb.

Illustrated by the Sanskrit. By C. H. PARKHURST, formerly of Williston Seminary; now pastor of the Madison Square Church, New York. 12mo. Cloth. 55 pages. Mailing Price, 40 cents; Introduction, 35 cents.

DESIGNED to familiarize the student with the earlier and the later forms, to show how the latter were corrupted from the former, and to introduce the student to comparative grammar.

Madvig's Latin Grammar.

Carefully revised by THOMAS A. THACHER, Professor of Latin, Yale College. 12mo. Half morocco. 515 pages. Mailing Price, $2.50; Introduction, $2.25.

WHATEVER may be the preferences for one or another manual of Latin grammar, the scholars of the country agree in regarding this as of the highest authority.

H. A. Frieze, *Prof. of Latin, University of Michigan:* As a grammar for reference, and for the cultivation of thorough scholarship in Latin, I think it unequalled.

The Adelphoe of Terence.

Carl Dziatzko's Text. Edited with stage directions by HENRY PREBLE, Instructor in Latin, Harvard College. Paper. 56 pages. Mailing Price, 30 cents; for introduction, 25 cents.

White's Junior Student's Latin-English Lexicon.

By the Rev. J. T. WHITE, D.D. (Oxford), Rector of St. Martin's, Ludgate, London. Revised edition. Square 12mo. 662 pages. Morocco back. Mailing Price, $1.90; Introduction, $1.75.

White's Junior Student's Latin-English and Eng-

lish-Latin Lexicon.

Revised edition. Square 12mo. 1053 pages. Sheep. Mailing Price, $3.30; Introduction, $3.00.

White's Junior Student's English-Latin Lexicon.

Revised edition. Square 12mo. Morocco. 392 pages. Mailing Price, $1.65; Introduction, $1.50.

CONVENIENT and accurate lexicons, sufficiently comprehensive for the use of junior students, and sold at low prices.

The Athenæum, *London:* The accurate scholarship and careful execution by which the work is distinguished are highly creditable to the editor.

The Nation: The etymologies are trustworthy, so far as we have been able to examine. There is nothing so good elsewhere.

An Etymology of Latin and Greek.

With a Preliminary Statement of the New System of Indo-European Phonetics, and Suggestions in regard to the study of Etymology. By CHARLES S. HALSEY, A.M., Principal of the Union Classical Institute, Schenectady, N.Y. 12mo. Cloth. 272 pages. Mailing Price, $1.25; Introduction, $1.12.

THIS work presents the subject in a systematic form, on a new and simple plan, giving great prominence to the derivation of English words, and serviceable as a class-book and for reference. This is the first schoolbook to set forth in English the new system of Indo-European Phonetics.

J. H. Heinr. Schmidt, *in the "Berliner Philologische Wochenschrift":* This work is characterized by a very convenient and practical arrangement. It holds throughout the system of etymology founded upon the latest phonetic views. It would be very desirable to have in the German language such a book, presenting for beginners a clear view of the subject.

Latin Text-Books.

CPSIA information can be obtained
at www.ICGtesting.com
Printed in the USA
BVOW06s2232081217
502294BV00013B/418/P